Finding Christmas

Tales and Poems of The Spirit of Christmas

Derek Becher

~~ *ACKNOWLEDGEMENTS* ~~

FOR MOM & DAD:
THANK YOU FOR TEACHING ME AND MY SIBLINGS ABOUT THE
TRUE REASON FOR CELEBRATING DURING THE CHRISTMAS
SEASON, AND FOR MAKING FAMILY SUCH A BIG PART OF IT.

FOR MOM:
THANK YOU FOR CREATING THE WONDERFUL ILLUSTRATIONS
TO ACCOMPANY MY CHRISTMAS STORIES AND POEMS.
WITHOUT THEM, MY DREAM OF CREATING AND PUBLISHING A
COLLECTION OF MY CHRISTMAS WRITINGS WOULD NOT HAVE
BEEN REALIZED.

FOR PEGGY MOEN:
THANK YOU FOR PUBLISHING AND SHARING MANY OF MY
CHRISTMAS WRITINGS OVER THE YEARS WITH YOUR READERS
OF THE *WANDERER*.

Table Of Contents

THE LAST DREAM

    62 Christmases he spent alone, after the year that his parents died, leaving him as an orphan. Each Christmas passed like just another day, another page falling endlessly from the calendar of his life. And all the while, in the privacy of his mind and his weakening heart, he hoped for something more, wished of something better. But with no family, and no one to call 'friend', he found it difficult to be touched by the wonder of the Christmas season, unable to even imagine how it would feel to spend the holidays with love.

    And so, with Christmas morning again less than twelve hours away, and his life's days now surely numbered, he arranged the loose papers to best find comfort on the hard wooden bench in the cold and the dark of this Christmas Eve, in the lonely, barren park he now calls home. The shoppers no longer hurried by on the nearby walks, and the silence began to beat in his mind. A cool numbing breeze swept through the tears in his ragged clothes, and the rhythm of his chattering teeth slowly dragged him into a deep, wintry sleep...

    He awoke in the comfort of a warm covered bed that he

shared with his loving wife, so beautiful as always, but even more so in sleep, in the glow of the morning sun. He followed the rays through the window outside where he noticed that snow had provided a soft, fresh blanket for the ground and had given pretty jackets to the tall evergreen trees stretching up the hills, into the mountains. Downstairs he could hear his children giggling in excitement about the gifts they would receive this night from dear Saint Nicholas.

After letting them nibble on hot buns with tasty sweet frosting, he took his little angels aboard his sleigh, drawn by his large black stallion, ever strong and sure, through the hills and into the forest where the smell of sweet, wet pine filled his lungs. And in a clearing, showered by the sun's golden rays, they found the perfect tree, her boughs plentiful and voluminous, which they brought home to decorate in merriment with the sounds of celebration and laughter filling their home. And just below her glorious branches, they gently placed the figures of their heirloom manger scene, glowing now in the twinkling lights of their wondrous tree.

Soon afterwards, they gathered their toques, mitts, and skates and strolled to the nearby frozen pond, which for years had provided him with many afternoons of familial joy and song. Together they skated and cheered for a long time into the late afternoon, until the light of the moon slowly emerged among the glistening stars. White crystals descended from the sky as they made their way home, half the way skipping, all the way singing!

Once home, upon entry, he paused as the aroma of his wife's wonderful cooking emanated from the kitchen. And there they gathered in thanks, enjoying a wonderful meal that made every taste bud dance with glee at the succulence of each tiny morsel. With a prayer following pudding, they gathered around the tree. And there, as always before, he read to his children the story of Christmas with the solemn melody of Silent Night playing softly behind, and he watched as their glittering eyes beamed with amazement.

Outside, pretty snowflakes swayed back and forth, swinging lightly to the ground, providing a winter blanket in the cold. Inside, warm from the heat of the flames dancing in the fireplace in synch with the crackle of logs below the neatly placed stockings, they smiled and began singing traditional carols that told of family and togetherness at Christmas, and of the hope brought by the birth of Jesus in a lowly manger in Bethlehem. And all the while he saw the wonder in the bright smiles of his beautiful children, and he felt the love in the eyes of his lovely, caring wife.

A feeling of peace shivered throughout his body, for he knew that the love of his family experienced in such cherished moments together, the warmth of his beautifully decorated home, and the joy of the peace and hope of Christmas provided him with the true meaning of his favourite season. So content on this holiest of evenings, he smiled, fulfilled, and sighed heavily...

This would be his last breath. The aging man, lonely and despairing, cold on the solitary park bench, passed away on the 24th of December as he had spent so many others - alone. He had known none of these feelings, these blessings he had somehow dreamed so lovingly of on his last Christmas Eve, for he never had a wife to love, a family to cherish, or a house to call home. But on this final holy night, alone beneath the Star of David, he received a gift that will carry him peacefully through eternity.

LI'L EVERGREEN

Li'l evergreen, you sparkle bright,
Enlightening dark winter's night;
Your shadows shed upon the walls,
And stretch among the house's halls.

For years I've set you in your stand
At Christmas, with a caring hand,
So you could fill my heart with cheer,
Making dark midwinter clear.

The tiny lights and balls you hold,
Glimmer green, red, blue and gold.
Your shiny needles - stretching long
Wish to dance with Christmas songs.

Your branches, some are crooked so,
But still, on you, the garland flows.
In my eyes, you're the finest tree
To place o'er my nativity.

For many days above the gifts
Your joy is spread, like snowy drifts;
Visitors throughout the season
Find your beauty truly pleasing.

The New Year now has come so fast;
So quickly, somehow, Christmas passed.
And though I pack you up, away,
I count now till next Christmas Day.

Li'l evergreen, you sparkle bright,
Enlightening dark winter's night.

THE EYES OF MEMORIES PAST

Ever since the first time I heard my father's cherished Christmas carols echoing softly throughout the cozy, softly glowing rooms of our small country home, when I was just a young child, something stirred inside, shivering my soul, that seemed to mean peace, and joy. I couldn't quite explain it, but it didn't matter, for it seemed so right and wonderful.

And now, listening to those same lovely harmonies in the comfort of my own home, I'm taken back to a fond childhood Christmas memory.

I'm there, sitting in wonder, listening to those familiar

sounds of Christmas, watching the smile, still on his face, as his happy but watery eyes look beyond the sparkling tinsel out into the falling snow, searching for a time he affectionately remembers and treasures. Dear Mother holds his hand, remembering with him, as we all sit silently with no need to speak, for the tranquility we feel with the soothing rhythm of those wondrous harmonies, reaching to the angelic glow atop the carefully trimmed tree, could not be shaken.

Each blink of his moist eyes brings a new memory of old as he's told so often, revisiting fond moments with his family on the farm in the dark of winter...

I see they're riding a sleigh, chiming bells into the woods with their terrier in tow, beyond the recently shovelled pond and fresh skate tracks, to search for that perfect tannenbaum in the depth of the forest. All the while they're laughing and singing favourite childhood carols, leaving trails of breath fading behind.

Upon return, the enticing aromas of fresh cooked goose and apple pie and gingerbread cookies and home-baked bread rise and float to every corner of the radiant dining area where they all soon gather in the merriment and the joy of each other's presence. And soon after they circle the gaily trimmed tree that brings light to the Bethlehem scene below, and they sing songs of joy as we do today.

Into the evening they ride the sleighs through the wintry white paths that wind through the valley - beneath the sparkling crystals that float from the heavens - toward the small steepled church amidst the towering pines. And there, once more, with the entire congregation, however small in number but still filling the church to almost bursting, they marvel at the glory of the story of Christ's birth. And they sing hymns of praise and thanksgiving, welcoming the wonder of that silent, holy night, where, away in a manger, the miracle of Jesus' birth in the lowly grotto, beneath the holy star in the city of David, brought hope for salvation to the world. And throughout the ceremony, the valley's life peeks through the frost-tinted windows and joins in the wonder of togetherness at Christmas below the twinkling sky.

With his eyes still searching, they're home once more, gathered as one. Sitting quietly together for a long moment, they drink in the peace and the wonder of Christmas, thankful for the love, the life, and the family that they share, before retiring to the warmth of their beds, to dream...

As he turns from the window to smile at Mother and their children, I know I've been blessed with a wondrous gift.

And now it is my family sitting in anticipation around our lovely decorated tree and home. Outside the snow continues to gently cover the darkened streets, and nothing else moves. Inside, the spirit of Christmas dances with our souls as we reminisce of favourite family Christmas memories, while forming new ones. It moves gracefully to those same treasured Christmas hymns as it did years before, skipping over the lips of my lovely wife and darling children.

Shortly, I will stand with the choir in the church in our town amidst family and friends - everyone - and sing joyously the hymns of Christmas. I hope one day that my eyes will show the memories of Christmas as my father's once did - of joy and simplicity, and the wonder of the beauty of the coming presence of the Lord as heard in what are now my favourite Yuletide carols. For then I know that my son will have seen the peace and the joy, the true meaning of Christmas, through the eyes of memories past.

THE MAGICAL JOURNEY

So many years have passed so quickly, quietly, somehow without notice. And though I've never returned to the wonderful, still countryside I called home throughout my youth, like yesterday, I remember being there, breathing, living there. And while my mind constantly strays to many of those marvelous memories, and my heart coincidentally feels the warmth of each, the fondest recollections I cherish now are of my childhood Christmases. Of these, the one I remember so vividly and right was our trip home every year from the Christmas Eve service.

Small though it was, our church was always full, particularly on Christmas Eve. Friends and relations from miles around would gather to warm the church with their presence; so much so that despite the clear chill sneaking in from the calm outdoors, inside together, we were wonderfully warmed as our hearts were filled with love and song. Closely we listened to the story of Christmas, and I often pondered how peaceful and serene it must have been that first holy night. Afterwards, we all gathered in the porch to both offer *and* receive Christmas blessings; and then, once bundled up, and one family at a time, we departed on separate journeys for welcoming homes. Secretly we were about to embark on my favourite journey, my favourite part of Christmas – I remember it well...

...With Christmas Eve slipping away, the stars dance and twinkle high overhead on the black canvas of the night sky. Father directs Hopper and Bells, though they know the way, and Mother, with hands tucked snuggly in her muffler, quietly slips into a peaceful slumber. Despite the chill, we children stay warm, cozily wrapped in our scarves and toques, snuggling together beneath the wool checkered blanket on the hay of our two horse sleigh. The church lights still beam through distant icy windows, but now fade slowly behind rolling hills and evergreen trees dressed in a thick coat of soft, white frost. The rhythmic breathing of my siblings means that they too are nearly asleep. As for me, my treasured Christmas present resumes.

Few lights greet our snowy path, which slowly winds nearly eight miles through Pinecone Valley; but the two candle lanterns attached to iron canes at the rear of the sleigh cast a soft golden glow that surrounds us, and the starry sky that blankets the earth – along with the bright sheen of the moon – provide more than enough light to lead us home. Ahead, the horses' breaths float upward, dissipating along tiny wisps of nothingness. All around, the evergreens grow thick and tall, and seem to enjoy each other's company, for they never stand alone. Sometimes they come up to and touch our trail, like friends along the way. Everywhere, the snow is pillowy soft, providing powdery warmth for the trees, and blanketing the ground. And a trillion little diamonds dance and run across the snow beneath the starry Christmas Eve sky.

Shushhh, the rudders glide over the snow. Mostly straight, our path gently rises and softly lowers, revealing new treasures behind each knoll, or from around an occasional corner. Slowly we cross the covered Ribbon Creek bridge, which is now adorned with wreaths of holly and bright red ribbons at both ends; closely below, the frosty creek curls and winds away over and around tiny hills to disappear into the trees. Forty counts later, as usual, we make a soft turn right, and dip into a tiny section of the valley where we always find the best tree for our Christmas home.

As we gently rise once more, I see snow crystals dancing between the stars and me. We cross a second bridge over Ribbon Creek, and I can see the tracks further up the hill where we sledded this morning. All around us, the friendly animals are nestling in their homes, except for the occasional deer or rabbit that skips out to greet us, pausing briefly to inhale the Christmassy air before returning to be with its family in its forestry home. Everywhere, the starry calmness of Christmas blankets the earth and, for one night at least, provides a feeling of infinite peace and joyful hope; and tiny hairs stand and dance along my arms as I shiver in the warm feeling I receive.

Faraway in the distance, at the end of a loop around a tiny frozen pond where we skated only several hours ago, I can faintly see the light of the shiny star we hung on our front gate, and the softly glowing bulbs trimming the eaves and windows of our home.

Mother still sleeps, and Father casts a quick glance back to peruse all his children, except me, quietly sleeping. With the gleam of an unusual star in his eye, he winks and again turns forward. The still silence I notice the most, so peaceful, so beautifully quiet, telling me that tonight the world embraces hope and joy, beneath our dark, starry skies. With maybe two hundred counts left to go, I feel comfortably alone in a tranquil glowing world, reliving a familiar moment of serenity in the glittering blue December night.

Slowly it's evolved before me; I know how it goes, but I never fail to feel the happiness and surprise of receiving each instant of such a precious gift. I bask in it, and know that before long, we will return to our home, so wonderfully decorated and warm, to sleep and dream of Christmas morning.

As we turn up our drive, I feel the mixed tingle of anticipation and calmness as I arouse from my conscious muse, the unfolding of a forty minute journey that I solitarily treasure in the quietude of Christmas Eve along our easy country trail. As the rest of my family awakens from a wintry nap, I am glad I stayed awake again to see and feel the serenity of Christmas...

We've all grown up now, and Mother and Father are gone, surely living every day now in the joy of the hopeful spirit of Christmas. Sadly, our old home is now but a house, sitting empty and crooked, and alone. But for the most precious years of my life, it marked the end of a magical journey that led us every Christmas Eve from a celebratory church service through the forest and hills of Pinecone valley, and over the wooden bridges of Ribbon Creek, through a period of time and a feeling that seemed to stand still, while I observed and pondered the peacefulness and the true meaning of Christmas.

HOME, FOR CHRISTMAS

It's nestled in fragrant and frost-covered pines,
Whose branches embrace the fresh feathery snow,
At the end of the drive beside pickets of white –
In the dark of the winter, the lone warming glow.

A thin wispy curl of cedar-sweet smoke
Flirts through the flue, and twirls to the sky;
And icicles dance down the eaves and the sills –
Frosty, frozen Christmassy sighs.

Nativity characters, softly-lit, glow –
A marvelous scene I remember so true;
With wandering tracks of the deer and fine fauna
Who share in the wonder of hope again new.

Birds whistle songs 'round the pine cones and needles,
While stars sparkle high – only they could have seen
The birth of a saviour, now so long ago,
So quietly peaceful, so softly serene.

Still calmness I feel, halcyon holy eve,
The crisp airy breath, I inhale so deep;
A memory emotion, I look to my window...
Envisioning warmth in my bed, where I'll sleep.

Our Christmassy home, ah the stories it holds,
So blessedly filled - warm laughter, love mild;
The music, though low, I can hear through the shelter.
I open the door, and again I'm a child.

JACOB'S GIFT

For an eight-year-old child, Christmas can be a time of wonder and excitement. With holiday music in every shop and in the wonderfully-decorated homes of your neighbourhood, sparkling wreaths attached to street lamp posts, strangers greeting each other with warm smiles, and, of course, dreams of Santa Claus, there is a magic in the air.

And for little Jacob, in the country village of NobleTown, with December flurries laying a soft white blanket throughout the gently rolling hills and woods, and modest decorations adding a colourful presence to the stores on Centre Street, it was no different. Still, having saved 10 dollars he had earned from clearing sidewalks and delivering the town newspaper, Jacob had something *else* to look forward to – the snow globe nativity that wound up and played *"Silent Night"*. He had seen it in the front window of the Country Gift Shop, and had decided that it would be the perfect gift for his parents. He was looking forward to seeing them unwrap it on Christmas morning, and during the last week of school, he waited anxiously for the start of the holidays, when he had planned to purchase it.

Jacob was now in Grade 3, and it had been an entertaining week at school. In Art class, the students were making Christmas wreaths, drawing nativity scenes, and creating their own stockings and trees. They filled their room with the spirit of Christmas, and looked forward to taking home their creations for the holidays. In Reading and Language, their teacher – Miss Pleasant – had been reading such tales as *"A Christmas Carol"*, *"The Night Before Christmas"*, and of course, the *"Story of the First Christmas"*, which she read from the bible. All week long the children sat still with wide eyes, listening attentively to the timeless stories.

During recesses and at lunch break, the principal played instrumental holiday music over the intercom, while children and teachers walked throughout the hallways, exchanging happy greetings and occasionally humming along to – or singing with – the melodies that flowed throughout the school. With everything that was going on, there was no mistaking what time of year it was, and for Jacob, and his Grade 3 classmates, it was a week filled with merriment and anticipation.

But this year, the season was even more special. Because he was in Grade 3, his class would now be taking part in the annual Christmas Pageant, held every year on the evening of the last Friday before Christmas. All week long, in addition to the crafts and the stories and the music that filled their days, Miss Pleasant's class was also preparing its skit for the Friday night festival. The sixteen students would be singing her favourite song – "*Silent Night*".

They had been practicing a simple arrangement which Miss Pleasant had fashioned: on the stage in the school gymnasium, the students would stand in a semi-circle pattern around two of their classmates who would kneel on the floor and hold a doll, representing the Christ child. Jacob had been granted the special role of playing Joseph, while his classmate, Sara, would be Mary.

For one period each day that week, Miss Pleasant took her Grade 3 class onto the stage for a private practice of their skit. She had planned for two students to enter at the beginning of the second verse as shepherds, to coincide with the words of the song; one of them would direct the light of a flashlight towards the doll's face, representing "*…love's pure light…*", at the beginning of the third verse. The students practiced diligently throughout the week, and by Friday, the day of their final rehearsal, the school principal arrived and applauded the class for a "wonderful performance that was sure to please everyone that night."

In the last period that day, Christmas music was again echoing throughout the halls of the school and into the classrooms. Miss Pleasant and her students spent the whole period playing games while enjoying Christmas oranges and candy canes. When the bell rang at the end of the day, she reminded her students to meet back in the classroom at 6:30, so that they could gather and prepare one last time for their 7:00 presentation. Wearing coats, toques and mittens, the students skipped out of the school beneath a gentle snowfall, and scattered away to their nearby homes.

Of course, Jacob fully enjoyed the festivities at school, but he was just as eager to purchase the special gift he had found for his parents. He imagined the joy it would bring them on Christmas morning, and he looked forward to wrapping it and setting it under the tree. He had planned to leave first thing Saturday morning for the Country Gift Shop.

Back in Miss Pleasant's homeroom, the students were returning one last time before the Christmas break, with an excited chatter and bright smiles on their young faces. In a few short hours, they would all be going home for a two-week celebration of Christmas, and the enthusiasm was evident in the Grade 3 room and throughout the school, as students and teachers were returning and hurrying to their classes to prepare for their performances. It was a feeling of excitement and anticipation that Jacob and his classmates had yearned for during their first two years at school, and at last, it was here for them to savour.

At ten minutes to 7:00, Miss Pleasant got her cue from the school principal and had her students line up quietly at the door. With exuberance spread across their faces, they followed her, one by one, down the hallway towards the back entrance to the stage. With the curtains still closed, they could hear a faint murmuring throughout the auditorium, and the occasional shuffle of a chair. Surely, everyone from NobleTown had again assembled to enjoy the annual pageant.

The children stepped quietly into their places. Jacob and Sara knelt in the centre, facing each other, near the front of the stage, dressed in their robes. Sara cradled a doll in her arms. The others formed a semi-circle around them, and two boys stood to the side in their shepherd garments, ready to enter the scene with the words of the second verse.

Miss Pleasant slipped through an opening in the curtains, introduced herself, and announced the song and short accompanying skit that her class would be performing. The auditorium lights dimmed as she returned behind the curtains. She gave a wink to her students, reached her tape recorder, and gave a nod to the curtain attendant. As the curtains spread apart, the neat arrangement of her students was slowly revealed, and Miss Pleasant pressed the play button on the recorder. An instrumental version of the familiar melody echoed softly throughout the room, and at the right moment, as they had rehearsed, the students began to sing "*Silent Night*".

Jacob and Sara alternately smiled at each other and towards the doll, humming along as they had practiced. The first verse was smoothly and flawlessly performed, and as the second verse began, the two shepherds entered the scene, appearing somewhat amazed at what they were seeing. As the third verse began, one of them directed the soft glow of a flashlight onto the doll's face.

Still smiling, it was then that Jacob gazed into the audience, and noticed two small children standing beside their mother at the back wall of the auditorium. They smiled meekly, as each clutched the limbs of a single, stuffed and tattered teddy bear. Through the length of the room, Jacob could see the flashlight's glow reflected in the teary eyes of the small boy and girl who stood there, smiling, appreciating the simple gift of song that they were receiving. Their clothes were ragged, but their hair was combed neatly, as their mother stood humbly beside them.

As the words of the final verse were being sung, a tear trickled down Jacob's face. NobleTown was not a wealthy community, but its people were happy, and they enjoyed a modest, country living. And yet, at the back of the room, three strangers stood, appearing needy, and unfortunate.

As the song ended, the members of the auditorium stood proudly and applauded the performance of Miss Pleasant's Grade 3 class. But as the curtains drew to a close, Jacob knelt with a lump in his throat. The students returned to their class, gave their teacher and each other a hug, and then left with their parents to celebrate Christmas. But after waving goodbye to his friends, Jacob sat at his desk, alone in thought. Miss Pleasant noticed him as she herself prepared to go home for the holidays. She sat in a chair beside him, and asked what could possibly be troubling the normally cheerful boy.

Jacob slowly explained what he had seen during their performance, and how it had affected him. Miss Pleasant comforted him, and mentioned that she had heard that morning that a new family had moved to town. The father had been injured, and was being cared for by his wife and his sister, his only remaining family. They were poor, but the father had worked hard cutting wood and creating various sculptures, until he fell off a ladder and broke his leg, and the two women were skilled in the craft of needlework. They moved into the empty aged house at the end of Centre Street just last night.

Jacob gave Miss Pleasant a hug and walked home. But as he lay in bed that night, he couldn't erase the image of the two children who stood at the back of the auditorium, apparently in need, yet wholly comforted by the gentle sound of the Grade 3 performance of "*Silent Night*".

In the morning, Jacob put on his coat, his boots, his mittens, and his toque, and put his ten dollars into his pocket, before leaving for the Country Gift Shop. But as he arrived at the front window, and saw the little snow globe inside, he remembered the two children from the auditorium. In front of him sat the most perfect gift that he thought he could give to his parents. But as he wandered in, and the little bells on the front door jingled, he saw another item sitting alone on a shelf in the corner. It was a furry, cuddly teddy bear, with light brown hair, fuzzy ears, and two big brown eyes that glistened and reflected his image. He remembered the tattered bear that the children both clung to, maybe a third as big as the one that sat in front of him.

Jacob looked at the beautiful big bear for a long time, and then again at the wonderful snow globe. He was torn between buying the musical globe for his parents, and seeing their pleased faces on Christmas morning, or spending his ten dollars on the furry, big teddy bear that would surely brighten the hearts of the children who stood quietly at the back of the auditorium, enjoying their simple gift of song. Sighing, Jacob picked up the teddy bear, gave the shopkeeper his money, and walked to the end of Centre Street.

He knocked on the door, and as it creaked and slowly opened, he saw the hopeful faces of the two children. He smiled at them, and brought the new teddy bear from behind his back and said, "Merry Christmas!" Their mother and aunt had seen his kind gesture, and their eyes became wet with happy tears. Jacob was invited inside, and he sat at a table with the family, enjoying a small cup of hot cocoa, and sharing a plate of home-baked cookies. So thankful for the gift that Jacob had presented to the younger children, the women gave him a new pair of blue mittens and a blue scarf for his mother. Both of these contained a pattern of white snowflakes of a variety of sizes. They were beautiful, and he knew his mother would love them. Then the father handed him a small wooden nativity set for his own father. It contained a manger and a variety of shepherds and animals that accompanied the Holy Family, all of which were intricately carved. He knew that his father would love the gift. Jacob also knew that the love that was put into creating these gifts would compensate for not being able to bring home the snow globe for his parents.

He left feeling gratified, having brought some joy to the new family, while returning with special presents for his parents. He began to wrap them as soon as he got home, and then he placed them under the tree. It was Christmas Eve, and even though he tried, he couldn't stay awake to greet Santa Claus during the night. He slept soundly, contented.

On Christmas morning, he hurried to the Christmas tree, where his parents soon joined him. Together, they said a prayer to bless the birth of Jesus, and then turned on some music. As they exchanged gifts, Jacob received new socks, a shirt, a game, and two toys from Santa, saving his last gift until his parents opened the special gifts he brought them. The mittens he brought for his mother fit her perfectly, and she looked beautiful in them, especially as she wrapped her new scarf around her neck. When she hugged him, they felt soft against his face. Then his father unwrapped the skillfully-crafted wooden nativity scene. He looked at it with wonder, hugged Jacob in thanks, and then placed it gently beneath their tree, where it would be set for years to come.

Finally, Jacob began to unwrap his last gift from Santa. His parents sat close on the chesterfield and watched as he pulled away the paper, filled with curiosity. As he peeled the last piece of tape from a small box, and removed the rest of the wrapping, Jacob lifted the box flaps and pulled apart the white tissue papers from inside. He pulled out an item from the box and looked at it with unbelieving eyes as he cradled it in his hands in front of him.

He was holding the little snow globe nativity, the same one he had seen at the Country Gift Shop. Somehow, he thought, Santa knew how much he loved the gift himself. Jacob turned it over, wound it up, and then set it back on the table. Tiny snowflakes fell on the nativity inside the globe, and "*Silent Night*" played along in harmony. He gazed at it, as his parents watched him with happy, loving eyes.

A tear of happiness appeared in Jacob's eye as he looked at and listened to his special gift. It had been quite a week – the excitement at school, his first Christmas pageant, befriending the new family in town, and a Christmas morning that he would never forget. He was only 8 years old, but Jacob had already learned of the spirit of Christmas, and it was a gift that would follow him the rest of his life.

CHRISTMAS EVE IN DAYDREAM VALLEY

Daydream Valley - oh what a place
of beauty, at Christmastime!
With rolling hills around Tiny Town,
and a blanket of snow, so fine!

There's a frozen pond, past the village square,
near the church's nativity scene;
And high overhead in the clear starlit sky -
the moon spreads a marvelous sheen!

It's Christmas Eve, and the valley is silent,
and children have fallen asleep;
And grown-ups are placing some treats near their trees...
for jolly old Santa to keep!

But out in the woods, on this wonderful night,
where the animals cuddle, to dream,
Miracle wonders descend from the sky -
on a starry celestial beam.

Guardian angels have gently arrived,
while their children are dreaming away;
And they're bringing a gift for their animal friends,
on the eve before Christmas Day.

They gather on pillows of snow, on the branches -
each angel a colourful light -
And they reach to hold hands, and then softly they carol
their version of "O Holy Night".

The animals rise, and then gather below
all the trees where the angels are singing;
Squirrels and rabbits and raccoons and deer
delight in the gift that they're bringing.

Oh, it's Christmas Eve, and once again,
the angels have come to rejoice;
And over the hills, from the sheltering woods,
spreads a wonderful, Christmassy voice.

But near in a den, in the light of the moon,
a doe winks its eyes to the world;
Returning a gift to their heavenly friends,
a tiny new life has unfurled.

A miracle's come in this still, silent night,
as in Bethlehem so long ago!
And angels and animals chorus the peace
that has blessed them this night, in the snow.

Then all join as one, in the calm of the woods,
and together they play and they prance;
While carolling hymns, singing "Joy to the World",
they mix and they mingle and dance!

A Christmas tradition: the angels have come,
bringing joy - although now they must leave,
To be with their children and share in the joy
of the day after Christmas Eve.

ANNA'S WISH

    Anna lay still on her hospital bed, which was tilted slightly upwards, while she slept. Her parents sat beside her, with their hands clenched together, sharing a prayer as they watched their only child labouring with each breath. She had only just turned 9, but the brave little girl had fought the dreadful disease with the fervor of a healthy adult, impressing her family and surprising her doctors with her will to live.

    Outside the window, snow fell gently in the December night. It was and always had been her favourite time of year. Anna loved the snow; she would lie in its softness and move her arms and legs to make perfect little snow angels. She loved the decorations; Anna marvelled at the colourful lights, the flowing ribbons and tinsel, and the lovely trees and wreaths that appeared in every home in her town during the Christmas season. Anna loved the music; starting in mid-November, she would play their holiday collection over and over, just sitting near their tree and wondering what a great world it would be if the music played the whole year through. But most of all, Anna loved the peace of the Christmas season - the stillness in the air, the way strangers greeted each other with friendly smiles and sincere holiday wishes, and the story of the first Christmas. She often dreamed what a calm, serene evening it must have been that night in Bethlehem, when the infant Jesus came into the world as the greatest gift of all. Indeed, Christmas had been one of Anna's reasons for living, and as the minutes ticked away in the early morning hours of December 24th, she secretly prayed that she would live to see one more Christmas Day.

As dawn broke, Anna's eyes opened to the smiling and comforting faces of her parents, who fought to hide their fear and sadness. Anna struggled to swallow some water as the breakfast hours came and disappeared, and through the afternoon, she slid in and out of a sleep that helped to ease the pain she had felt during these last weeks.

The afternoon advanced, though each moment felt like a lifetime for Anna's parents, as they watched hopelessly as their child's light dimmed before them. Darkness fell again and seemed to suck the very light out of their room, through the window. Anna woke for a time, smiling especially when she noticed a light snowfall outside the window; it was a perfect Christmas Eve, she thought. And then, with the strength that had often surprised her doctors, Anna spoke softly to her parents, happily remembering her few past Christmases, and sharing her favourite memories with them. From the colourful decorations, to the wonderful music, to the fun outside in the snow, to singing Christmas carols together, and to the surprise of Christmas morning, Anna recalled Christmas moments like they had happened just yesterday. Her parents were astonished with her memory, and their eyes dampened with tears as they too remembered the Christmas moments they had fondly shared with their daughter.

Anna then surprised them with a question, asking, "Daddy, is there a Santa Claus in Heaven?" He looked deeply into her eyes as both he and his wife gently held their daughter's hands. After thinking for a moment, he said, "Of course, Anna. Santa is everywhere, and he brings joy both to children on earth *and* in Heaven. He'll be so happy to see you," he added, with a lump in his throat.

Anna closed her eyes as her beautiful smile lit up the discolouration that the disease had brought to her once bright, young face. Truly, she beamed with the thought of meeting Santa. She lay back then and fell asleep.

Just then, the green line that had alternately zigzagged up and down on the monitor beside her bed stayed flat, and a steady beeping sound filled the room. Anna's parents wept as they realized what had happened, also knowing that their daughter would not experience the excitement of another Christmas morning.

Like a dream, Anna felt herself walking down a long hallway. With her hospital gown still on, she looked like an angel as she disappeared into the glow of a white light, with the feeling of peacefulness sweeping through her. As she emerged from the other side of the light, a man approached her, wearing a white, flowing robe. A thick, but neat beard covered his face, and his eyes shone with a loving gentleness. As he approached her, Anna asked the man, "Mister, are you Santa Claus?" He smiled at her innocent question, and with a soft voice, he replied, "My child, there *is* a Santa in Heaven, but I am not that man. He has a *white* beard, you see, and his outfit is red. But he *is* a friend of mine, since we both love to bring joy to children."

Anna smiled then, knowing who the man in front of her was. But her eyes lit up even more, as He said, "Hold my hand, and come with me. I have a present for you." In an instant, Anna found herself standing alone outside a crowded inn, near a simple, wooden manger. A gathering of animals either stood or lay in front of her, and she heard the gentle cooing sound of a baby. Its mother and father knelt beside its crib, which was filled with straw and covered with a thin blanket. As a bright star gleamed high above them, Anna realized she was witnessing the first Christmas. All around the world from which she had just come, people were arising to celebrate the very event that she was now observing. Quietly then, after gently petting each of the animals, Anna walked up to the crib, bent over, and gave the child a soft kiss on the forehead. Mary and Joseph smiled at her, nodding, and she then backed away to let them admire their little boy.

Anna then found herself again standing at the end of the hallway. Behind her, the bright light continued to glow, and in front of her, the friendly man with the beard stood calmly, smiling. As he looked down upon her, the man said, "Anna, your heart is filled with love, but your body is ill; still, your love for children and for animals is needed in the world. I love you and I'll miss you, but I want you to go back to your parents; they need your inner strength. Please, keep Christmas in your heart, as you always do, and share its beauty with everyone you meet. You will wake again in your hospital bed, and before long, you will be healthy once more. Remember, I am always with you; help the needy children of the world to learn this, too."

With those words, and his caring smile, Anna felt herself moving backwards down the hallway, disappearing beyond the glowing white light. At the same moment, the steady beeping sound that accompanied the solid green line on the monitor beside her bed once again became interrupted with pauses of silence. Just a few moments after hanging their heads in grief, Anna's parents turned quickly from the bed and stared at the monitor, with disbelief. They then felt a barely noticeable squeeze from the fingers of their daughter's hands, which they still held. They turned towards her face in time to see her eyelids flicker, while at the same time, just minutes after midnight, she softly offered a faint, "Merry Christmas."

It was a Christmas miracle in the truest sense. Anna's secret prayer to see one more Christmas Day had been answered; indeed, she had seen and felt the serenity of the most blessed of Christmas Days, just as she had imagined, and now she had been granted many more. Her parents hugged their daughter joyfully, together, and they rejoiced at the best gift they could have received that special Christmas morning.

Together, they spent Christmas in the hospital, and it would be many days before Anna would recover enough to go home. But true to the man she met in Heaven, Anna grew up to care for children, and she brought four of her own into the world. And every Christmas Eve, with her little ones snuggled beside her, Anna told the story of the first Christmas, without a book; for she had been there, and the memory stayed clear with her, forever.

GARLANDS IN THE SKY

The winter winds blew early that year, bringing a record snowfall to Jubilee County. By November, the country roads were impassable, as frosty drifts gathered and grew along the roadsides, especially where the woods crept towards their shoulders. A week later, country residents had already assembled their horse-drawn wagons and sleighs for the first trips into town, which became less frequent because of the duration of the round-trip excursion to MerryVale. Winter had indeed arrived early, and with the thick blanket of snow that it had brought, it was there to stay.

For Marie and her brother, Matthew, that first snowfall brought dreams of Christmas, as always. Before long, their town would be decorated with the symbols of the season. Twinkling candles and shiny wreaths would adorn street posts; frosty snow and elaborate holiday images would bring colour to the inside of storefront windows; the town Christmas tree would again be wrapped with colourful lights, decorated with tinsel, and topped with an angel; and the wooden nativity scene would again be set at the front of Town Hall, welcoming visitors from everywhere. Together, they loved the beauty and the colour of the Christmas season, and they savoured every opportunity to wander through town, becoming immersed in the splendour.

As November progressed and eventually drew to a close, Marie became excited with the thought of a Christmas present she had planned to buy for her parents. Hers was a simple family, and money for decorations and lights and fancy ornaments just wasn't part of the family budget. But Marie had convinced the town's merchants that she could clean their sidewalks every morning and after school, if necessary, and she even offered to deliver their weekly flyers. In exchange, she would be able to earn the money she would need to buy her secret gift – a Christmas wreath. She had seen it hanging in the window of the town department store. It was a glorious wreath, thick with evergreen foliage, and it cradled a gathering of bright red holly berries, acorns, walnuts, and even a few fine strands of tinsel. In its middle sat an arrangement of 3 plastic candles of differing heights. "Oh, how this would beautify our home," Marie thought, realizing too that it would bring a touch of Christmas nature into their home that year. They always put up a tree, but it was always bare, except for a few strings of popcorn. Now she would be able to add some sparkle, light, and decoration to their Christmas experience.

For 4 weeks, Marie rode into town atop her father's

sleigh, bundled up in her winter clothing early in the chill of a winter morning, sharing her secret only with her brother Matthew. When she was dropped off at school, she would run into her classroom – always the first to arrive – to set her books and lunch bag on her desk. Then, she returned down the front sidewalk from the school and hurried along the block to Main Street. Quickly, but properly, Marie would clear the snow and ice from the sidewalks in front of the shops along the two blocks of Main Street, always pausing in front of the department store to admire the wreath, which seemed to sparkle as it reflected the colourful lights that surrounded it. Occasionally, Matthew accompanied her and followed behind with a broom as she pushed the snow with her wooden shovel. It was a short labour of love that they performed every morning that snowy December, and they always finished to the grateful "Thank-you's" of the storekeepers, and returned to school in time for their first classes.

Often, the snow continued throughout the day, and Marie and her brother would return after their last classes. Again, they'd clear the walks, finishing in time to now enjoy the colourful lights and decorations that shone along the street in the darkening sky. Across the street from them, the town Christmas tree stood proudly, spreading its colours throughout the yard in which it stood, and beside it, the lovely nativity scene glowed behind the yellow and blue floodlights that sprayed it. It really was a sight worth appreciating. Still, they always made their way back to school in time for the 5:00 rendezvous with their father, who was unaware of the extracurricular work that they were involved with.

At last, Christmas Eve arrived, and Marie and Matthew rose excited, looking forward to their final day in school before the holidays. Their mother was already baking fresh buns and gingerbread cookies as they sat for breakfast, and the delicious aromas filled their home. Marie looked up to an empty space on the wall beside their kitchen, across from the window, and pictured how perfectly the wreath would fill that spot.

As the children quickly finished, and put on their winter clothing, they bid farewell to their mother and joined their father outside, where he was already preparing the sleigh.

A light snow fell as they rode into town, and Marie whispered for Matthew's help to clear the walks, one last time. They dropped their things off at school, and Matthew joined his sister as she hurried to Main Street. When they finished the walks, Marie collected the money that she had earned from the shopkeepers, and counted 8 dollars in her hands. She looked at Matthew and exclaimed, "I did it! I have enough money to buy that beautiful wreath that's in the front window of the department store!" Matthew simply smiled, pleased that he was able to help his sister, and skipped along with her as she grinned all the way back to school.

Both of the children took part in Christmas celebrations in their classrooms that day, and spent the whole time playing with their friends, singing, and listening to music and to stories of Christmas, and enjoying candy treats and fudge that their teachers brought in. Marie secretly spied the clock often throughout the day, till at last, after all their celebrating, the bell rang at 3:15.

Marie had one thought in her mind as she stepped out of the school, and as soon as she found Matthew, she hurried to the department store. For 4 weeks she had cleared the walks along Main Street, all the while imagined the colour and beauty she would be able to give to her parents. At last, she would have the wreath, and her Christmas dream would unfold.

They hurried down the first block of Main Street, crossed the road, and arrived at the front of the department store. Marie looked up with anticipating eyes for a final view of her treasure; but she stopped in her tracks, and her jaw fell open in disbelief. The Christmas wreath, with its berries, candles, acorns, walnuts, and tinsel, was gone! She anxiously pulled the front door open, and Matthew followed her as she rushed in. She held on to a hope that perhaps the wreath had only been moved, but the shopkeeper confirmed her worst fear when he said, "Sorry, Marie, but someone came in this afternoon and bought that wreath; it was my last one. I wish I'd known you wanted it."

Marie's world seemed to crash in front of her. Gone was the hope for a bright and colourful Christmas home. Gone was the gift that she worked so long for, so hard for, to buy for her parents. Matthew followed her as she walked slowly out the front door.

They crossed the street and sat on a bench beside the town Christmas tree. Marie looked up at the empty window across the street, and began to softly cry. "What will I give my parents now," she wondered.

A moment of silence followed; but Matthew turned to his sister, then, and said, "Marie, do you remember what the priest said in church last week? He said, 'Remember that Christmas is Jesus' birthday.' Maybe you could give something to Jesus?"

Marie looked at her little brother, and paused, to clear her mind. Then, a sparkle seemed to appear in her teary eyes as a tingling feeling swept through her. Looking in his eyes, she sighed, then smiled, and said, "You're right, Matthew. Maybe there's a better way I can spend this 8 dollars."

With a new-found hope, Marie held her brother's hand,

and together, they walked down the street to the little church at the end of the road. As they stepped inside, they saw Father Joseph preparing for the Christmas Eve service. After he welcomed them, Marie explained everything that had happened – how hard she had worked; how long she had waited; how much she had looked forward to seeing the colourful wreath brighten their home for the Christmas season. Marie then told the priest that she wanted to give him the 8 dollars, and maybe he could find someone who needed the money more than she thought she did.

Father Joseph smiled and said that a special collection was being made that night for needy families in the world. He would put her 8 dollars in the collection during the mass. Before he let the children leave, though, he brought them an ivory-coloured Christmas candle that was part of a collection that had been stored in the church. It was a foot high, and Marie needed to use both hands to reach her fingers around it. Engraved in the middle of the candle was a picture of the infant Jesus in a manger, with Mary and Joseph beside Him. As Marie looked at it, she realized that this simple candle would bring all the colour and light to their home that they could want. Indeed, it would truly brighten their Christmas season!

Before they left, Father Joseph added, "Jesus will be so happy for this gift you are giving. Indeed, your heart is filled with the true spirit of Christmas."

After thanking the priest for his gift, Marie wrapped the candle in some tissue he had given her, and walked out the front door of the church with a wide smile on her face. By now, the sky was dark, and the colours of Main Street glowed around her. She returned to school with Matthew, and waited only a short while until their father arrived. As they rode on the back of the sleigh all the way home, the clouds that had brought a light snowfall earlier that day had disappeared and been replaced by a black, starry sky, the first one Marie had seen that month.

Inside, after they finished their supper, Marie carefully set the Christmas candle under the tree, still wrapped in its tissue. She looked forward to Christmas morning when her parents would unwrap it, sure that they would love it. As she pondered the surprise that would appear on her parents' faces, a soft, colourful glow slowly danced on the wall behind her. She looked up to see where it was coming from, and through the window, the northern lights shimmered in the clear night sky.

"Mom! Dad! Matthew! You have to come see this," she said, excited.

As her family gathered with her by the window, a rainbow of colours flowed and mingled among the stars, twinkling on the white blanket of snow below. Some of them appeared to flicker red, some green, and others blue and yellow, while a silvery line along the edge of the northern lights appeared to drape along some of the stars, like a long, unfurling piece of tinsel. Colourful garlands were streaming in the sky, even more beautiful than the wreath Marie had planned to buy, and they stayed there, dancing, throughout the night, providing a wonderful display that shone through the window, skipping and rolling along the very spot on the wall where the wreath was to hang. Marie's mother brought hot cocoas for everyone, and they sat together by the window, enjoying the Christmas Eve garlands in the sky while listening to both sides of their two albums of Christmas melodies. It was a magical Christmas moment that the entire family would remember – and treasure – forever.

Marie smiled as she lay in bed later that Christmas Eve,

thankful for the colourful lights that filled her home, providing her family with a wonderful and surprising decoration. But as she fell asleep, she was even more thankful that the wreath disappeared from the department store window. With some help from her brother Matthew, she learned that giving from the heart was the purpose of Christmas, and she found a gift that would bring her more peace and harmony than a thousand wreaths could ever have.

I SAW AN ANGEL

I saw an angel on the sill,
The dawn of Christmas Day;
It gazed upon my little crèche
And pressed its hands to pray...

Her whispered words were weaving
Into frost upon the pane;
It printed pretty lyrics
That the seraph would proclaim.

And then she strummed a little harp,
So smoothly, gently, there;
And then I heard her softly sing
This lovely little prayer:

"Little baby in the crib
I'll guard you ever so;
Baby Jesus, I'm with you
Wherever you will go."

She smiled so serenely, then,
Her face a lovely sight,
And fluttered to the heavens
In the Christmas morning light.

I saw an angel on the sill,
One blessed Christmas morn;
She sang a little Christmas prayer
When Christ our Lord was born.

THE SECOND-GREATEST GIFT

"She's gone, Thomas. I'm sorry."

With a hug, the words fell softly from Lisa's lips as she walked out of the operating room, her own eyes reddening from the moisture of salty tears. Yet, despite the enduring empathy that she showed and offered through these past few months, the words still sounded like an alarm to Thomas, and certainly, they felt like tiny daggers, tearing his heart apart. His beloved Annabella, who just a year ago was overflowing with a love for life, and energy, had ultimately breathed her last, succumbing to the disease that she had valiantly fought, despite the pain it caused her.

And now, mere days before Christmas, Thomas sat crumpled over in his familiar chair outside the operating room, with his head in his hands, wondering what more he could have done. He was with her every step of the way, caring for her, loving her, somehow bringing hope – and joy – into her life, even as she knew she was dying. He thought of how long he had searched for someone to join him in his journey through life. But still, he could not believe his fortune when he met Annabella, as they separately wandered along his favourite trail through the forests along the outskirts of town, before meeting each other, and beginning a wonderful, albeit short life together.

With his torn and heavy heart, Thomas stood up onto his still-trembling legs, offered a grateful hug to each of the nurses, doctors and auxiliary staff members who had generously offered their support and comfort, especially during the last few weeks, and then walked out the front doors of the hospital for the last time, into a gentle snowfall. On his way home, Thomas thought only of Annabella, and of the blessings she had brought to him. Her beautiful smile; her wonderful sense of humour; the sound of her laughter; her love for children and for family; her love for nature and for being in the surroundings of nature; her concern for the sick, the elderly, and the unfortunate. Indeed, Annabella had brought fulfillment and completeness to Thomas' life far beyond what he had ever dreamed. He had often felt that she was an angel who had appeared to join him in his journey, and truly, her heart and her soul were pure, and loving.

But now, as he walked along the snowy streets towards his home, a dark emptiness filled his soul, as Thomas realized that he was again alone, and the one and only true love of his life – his dear Annabella – was gone, just days before Christmas.

The day of the funeral came – the second saddest day of his life. In the midst of a season when his heart should be filled with joy, and peace, and hope, despair instead clouded Thomas' mind and filled his heart, as he said his last farewell to his life's love. At home that night, the last one before Christmas Day, Thomas held his favourite picture of his lovely wife tight in his hands, and hugged it close to his chest. Despite his sadness, he let the sounds of the Christmas hymns that they cherished together, play from the stereo in the living room. A tiny flame flickered in front of him while he sought any kind of comfort, sitting close to the fireplace.

"Oh, Annabella…" he whispered with a quavering voice, "I love you so deeply. You were the greatest gift I ever received, and I was so blessed to find you, and to have you in my life. Why did He have to take you – especially now?" With a pause, he added, "How will I get through Christmas, and through life, without you?"

The tears on Thomas' cheek glistened in the light of the slowly fading fire. He wrapped himself in a blanket, curled up tightly with Annabella's picture, and let his sorrow draw him into the mediocre relief of sleep.

The fire's flames gave way to a shimmering glow that cast shadows throughout the room from the hot embers at the bottom of the fireplace, and songs of the season still echoed softly as Thomas fell deeper and deeper into sleep, still clutching his beloved's picture. His breathing was more rhythmic now, and at last he let go of his sadness and his anguish long enough to allow his weary mind to fall into the relaxation of a dream, a place in sleep that he hadn't visited for more than a year.

Just then, a soft voice entered the room, and called for

him, "Thomas? Thomas, can you hear me?" Thomas turned slightly in his chair, still wandering in his subconsciousness. The voice came again, this time saying, "Thomas. It's me, Annabella."

Thomas' eyes snapped open wide, as he sat for a moment in light-headed confusion. Again, the voice came, "Hello, Thomas. It's me."

Thomas turned his face away from the chair's cushioned back and looked across the room. Standing on the hearth of the fireplace, silhouetted by the glow of the embers, was Annabella. She smiled at Thomas, and extended her hands towards him.

It was approaching midnight, near the end of Christmas Eve, as Thomas looked with bewilderment at his beautiful Annabella. "Don't be afraid," she said, as she stood in a lovely flowing white robe that was stitched in red and drawn closed by a silky green sash.

"But...but...," he tried to put his thoughts together to speak to her, as his reddened eyes watered once more.

Annabella stepped forward, still enveloped by a soft glow, and took hold of Thomas' hands, helping him up to her. He embraced her and held her as he always did, saying, "I love you Annabella."

She simply smiled, replying, "I know, Thomas. I love you too, and I always will."

As Thomas held her, he told her how, in his heart, he fought to welcome the joy of Christmas – their favourite season – but that he felt so hopeless without her. Together, they were blessed with three wonderful Christmases spent in the comfort of their home, continuing traditions they brought from their families, and starting new traditions of their own.

He fondly remembered the Advent calendars they had created, with openings revealing pictures of happiness they shared throughout the year, and wishes they had in their hearts for Christmas and for peace in the coming year. He remembered the Christmas Eve prayer they said each year as they knelt side by side at the foot of their tree, gently placing the wooden figures of their nativity below a lone, softly glowing yellow light. But the most cherished remembrance of Christmas that he shared with Annabella, as he stood looking at her in the dimly-lit room while holding the delicate skin of her soft hands, was the tradition they started at their first Christmas. It was Annabella's idea, and Thomas wholeheartedly agreed when she suggested that they stop by the children's ward of the hospital that Christmas Eve. They brought gingerbread cookies that they baked together that morning, and when they arrived, they read the Christmas Story to the children. Afterwards, they sang Christmas carols that the children chose, and then passed around the delicious treats as all the children delighted in the gift of joy that they received.

"Yes, Thomas, I also treasure all of these," Annabella said, as she held the calendar that Thomas made for her a few weeks earlier, when she lay dying in her hospital bed. "And this is why I'm here," she added.

Thomas frowned with curiosity, wondering what Annabella was referring to. But before he could ask, she led him towards their tree, and they knelt down together in front of the manger.

"Thomas," she said, "I have a prayer for us to say tonight that was given to me by a very wonderful lady. Our Holy Mother, Mary, gave this to me, and she asked that we read it together."

Annabella pulled a slip of paper from the pocket of her
robe, and along with Thomas, they read:

*"Dear Jesus. Thank you for the gift of joy that you bring us each
Christmas. Help us to share this joy with the children of the world,
who need it most."*

Together, they knelt for a few moments in silence, staring
at the infant Jesus in the manger below them.

As he turned to her, Annabella smiled, and said,
"Thomas, please know that I am always with you, and I always
will be with you. I know that your heart hurts right now, and it
will. But you must find a way to fill this void by bringing joy to
those who most need it. When you do this, your own heart too
will be blessed with the joy of Christmas."

They sat on the chair together, as they held each other
tightly, sharing the warmth of the coals and the soft melodies of
their favourite carols. Like so many times before, in the comfort
of each other's arms, they rested peacefully, and fell asleep.

Thomas woke in the morning light of Christmas Day.
Remembering his dream, he looked for Annabella, but found
himself still clutching her picture, as he had before he fell
asleep. As the angel that he always thought she was, Annabella
came to Thomas in his time of grief and comforted him,
promising to always be with him, and even showing him how
to deal with his sorrow.

Thomas sat up in his chair, realizing he had something to
do on this Christmas Day. Before long, three dozen gingerbread
cookies sat cooling on the counter, and the sweet spicy aroma
filled his home. Thomas gently stacked the cookies in a

cardboard box. Then he found his illustrated "*The Story of The First Christmas*", gathered some song sheets, and then dressed warmly before entering the outdoors for the walk to the hospital. The soft snowfall that came throughout Christmas Eve left the ground and the trees glistening beneath a crisp, clear blue sky.

As he walked to the hospital, Thomas remembered the encounter he had with Annabella, as he dreamed on Christmas Eve. He still sorely missed her, and he felt that he would long for her smile, her laughter, and mostly, her love, for the rest of his life. But he also knew that during their time together on earth, Annabella loved him deeply, and on the holiest, most peaceful night of the year, she returned to offer Thomas the one gift that he needed most. At the depth of his despair, Annabella promised – and had already proven - that she would always be with him, thereby providing him with the gift of hope. Moreover, by starting a special tradition with him, and by leading through her own example, Annabella then reminded Thomas that his gift for song, and his genuine concern and care for children and for the less fortunate – that they both shared – would lead him towards replacing his grief with the fulfillment of giving of himself, and the opportunity to make the world a better place for those who most needed it.

Thomas paused in front of the crèche that sat in the freshly fallen snow near the front of the hospital. Inside, he saw the loving looks on the faces of Mary and Joseph, and the peaceful smile on the face of the infant Jesus. He remembered the prayer that he said with Annabella, "…*Help us to share this joy with the children of the world, who need it most*."

At that moment, the church bells at the end of the block began to ring out "*Joy to the World*". As he looked at the baby Jesus, Thomas smiled for the first time in weeks, realizing that the return of the Christ child that Christmas morning symbolized the ultimate gift of joy and hope that the world ever received. Knowing that Annabella was sharing the moment with him, he whispered a faint, "Thank you, Annabella."

In his heart, Thomas actually *did* feel a touch of joy, as the spirit of Christmas momentarily replaced the sorrow that had filled his soul for so long. With his cookies, his storybook, and his song sheets, Thomas stepped through the front doors of the hospital, where he continued a tradition that would last his lifetime.

Every year after, in the midst of the joy of the Christmas season, the one time of the year when Thomas most missed his beloved Annabella, she would return to him in dream, to remind him of how much she loved him. And as Thomas returned to the hospital each Christmas Day, he saw Annabella's love in the bright smiles of the children who shared laughter and song, and he received the gift of hope, knowing that her love enabled him to share of himself in order to brighten the lives of the hospital children. The gift he received from the children – letting him give of himself – inspired by the love of his dear Annabella, turned out to be the second-greatest gift that Thomas would ever receive.

THE ANGEL CHOIR

While cradled in his mother's arms,
With lowly sounds from creatures near,
And father Joseph watching humbly
In a cave, with mild revere,

The infant Jesus – from a manger –
Rests, with shepherds watching nigh,
And smiles, slightly, to the sounds
Of angels singing praise, nearby.

He's lulled to sleep with lullabies
Of sweet and peaceful harmony,
As angels from the star above
Exalt the child with melodies.

The gentle play of violins
Adds perfect pitch to angel songs;
And gentle fingers strum a harp,
Leading joyful sounds along.

A tiny organ's blended in,
And holds the notes in steady tone,
While trumpets help declare the joy –
In tender hands, they're softly blown.

A flute perfects the mingling sounds,
With gentle lips, its play is pure.
The orchestra is now complete,
And sings its praise with low allure.

Through early light, the angels croon;
Their lovely voices carry, mild.
The shepherds, with their sheep, lay still
On matted hay, about the child.

The Holy Family rests with peace,
While Mary ever gently sways
In rhythm with the soothing sounds
Throughout the dawn of Christmas Day.

Morning breaks, and Jesus wakens.
Smiling to the angels, pleasant,
He thanks them for their gift of song,
The first, endearing, Christmas present.

CHRISTMAS BELIEVING

Elizabeth slowly walked down the steps from the front door of her school. She was one of the last students to leave on this, the final day of classes before Christmas. Normally, she was one of the first to spring out the front doors with her friends, especially during December, with all the excitement of Christmas in the air. But this year, Elizabeth stayed later so that her friends and classmates would leave before her, and not notice the tears that streamed down her face.

She was in Grade 4, and there had been so much excitement in her school during these last weeks before Christmas, as always. Christmas music echoed throughout the halls during recesses, lunch breaks, and after school every day since December began. Every class in the school had prepared songs or skits which they performed in the school's annual Christmas Ceremony. Elizabeth's teacher lit the appropriate candles of her classroom's Advent wreath every morning at the beginning of the first class, and followed it with a short prayer. The students designed their own Christmas cards to present to their parents this year, and, on this last day before Christmas break, they participated in a "Secret Santa" exchange of small gifts with each other. There was so much excitement and activity going on that Elizabeth shouldn't have had a reason to try to stifle tears on her way home for Christmas with her family.

But something had happened this morning that was a good enough reason to bring the glistening tears that now rolled down her rosy cheeks in the December air. After coming in from the mid-morning recess, Elizabeth was hanging up her coat and placing her boots on the large shoe shelf, beside some Grade 5 and 6 students. Not meaning to eavesdrop, she heard the older students talking about Christmas and the presents they were hoping to receive this year. What they were about to say left Elizabeth all at once surprised, disappointed, and confused.

"Remember when we thought that Santa Claus was the person who brought us presents each year? So much of that story is impossible; it's amazing we fell for it!"

The older students proceeded down the hall to their classrooms, not knowing that Elizabeth had heard them. She stood weakly beside the rows of boots, all alone, with a heavy heart and tears welling in her eyes.

"How could this be," she thought, regaining enough strength to walk slowly to her classroom, careful to arrive before the bell. The words that she overheard the older kids saying played over and over in her mind, and they would all day, leaving her unable to fully enjoy the festivities that continued right until 3:15.

"There *must* be a Santa Claus," she thought, "or we wouldn't get gifts every year? I don't understand. Mother and Father have told me all along about Santa Claus, and now I hear that he may not exist, and likely never has. What am I to believe?" Elizabeth was clearly shaken.

And then, Elizabeth thought of something even worse. She was a fortunate child, for she lived in a loving home, and her family always had the things that it most needed; most of the other kids in the neighbourhood were just as fortunate. But Elizabeth had learned of things in school, and she was empathetic towards children who weren't as fortunate as she was.

"There are so many poor and needy children in this world," she thought. "Orphaned children. Children with no homes, or food, or families, or hope. If the older kids are right, what gifts do *these* children receive at Christmas, and how do they find joy or hope during the season?"

The confusion and desperation troubled Elizabeth even later as she sat for supper with her family. Fighting to smile, and, to more importantly hide her sadness, she asked to be excused as soon as she finished eating. Elizabeth spent the evening alone in her room, and she eventually slipped into bed early on one of the shortest nights of the year. With so much going through her mind, Elizabeth soon fell asleep listening to the sound of her parents' Christmas music playing down the hall in the living room, where a wonderfully-decorated tree stood majestically among the lights and garlands. What she didn't know, though, was that, despite her sadness and confusion, the dream she was about to experience would provide her with all the answers she would need to fill this Christmas, and all the rest of them, with peace, hope, and joy.

Elizabeth was soon sleeping deeply, emotionally exhausted from everything that had happened that day. It was this deep sleep that made her dream so vivid, and real....

She was sitting alone on a small bench, in a garden of thick green foliage and plants, behind a large stone church. However, still remembering the previous day, Elizabeth quietly sobbed, with her face in her hands.

In front of her, in the middle of the enclosed garden, she looked up, and through her teary eyes, she noticed a tall stone statue of a bearded man whose head was covered with a hood. He had a large sack over his shoulder, and he was guarding several children who stood closely around him. Elizabeth wondered why it appeared that the children loved this man so much; but she was soon interrupted by a gentle man who saw her tears through the thick wavy hair on his face, and how she admired the statue.

"Child, would you like to learn of this man," he asked, as he placed his hand softly on her shoulder. Elizabeth felt warmth from his touch, and immediately felt safe and comforted in his presence.

"Please sir," she started, "he looks so gentle, and so caring. Do tell me about him."

The bearded man sat beside Elizabeth on the bench, and began a tale that, even through dream, would change her life forever.

"This wonderful man is known around here as St. Nicholas, and there are many stories that are told of him. I will tell you these stories, so that you might learn of him.

"One story is that St. Nicholas once saved three daughters from lives of slavery. Long ago, a young woman's father had to offer something of value in order to attract a husband for his daughter. The more he could offer, the better chance his daughter would have of finding a worthy husband. With nothing to offer, though, a family's daughter would often be sold into slavery."

"That's terrible," exclaimed Elizabeth, worried about the daughters in his story.

"Fear not, my child," he replied, "for there is a happy ending to the story. To save these girls from lives of slavery, St. Nicholas arrived on three different occasions with a bag of three gold balls. Each time, he tossed the bag through an open window, and it landed in a stocking that was drying in front of the fire. He didn't reveal himself to the family, but these unselfish, caring gifts from St. Nicholas helped each daughter to attract a worthy, loving husband. St. Nicholas truly enjoyed the warmth he felt from helping those in need, and from giving from the heart. Henceforth, this caring man has been known as a gift-giver."

"That was very considerate of this man," replied Elizabeth, impressed by the generosity of the figure that stood, immortalized, in the centre of the garden.

"Ah, yes," the man continued, "but St. Nicholas was more than a caring, generous individual who gave gifts. You see, child, this wonderful man was also known as the person who guided all of those who travelled, especially by sea."

"Why is that," Elizabeth inquired, begging to hear the

next story from the gentle, bearded man, as her teary eyes began to dry.

"Elizabeth, when Nicholas himself was young, he travelled to the Holy Land, so that he could more deeply experience the life, passion, and resurrection of Jesus. Upon his return, a treacherous storm threatened to sink the ship that he was sailing in. As the terrified sailors ran about frantically doing everything to try to save themselves, Nicholas, who was devoted to a life of prayer - and to Jesus - feared not. Instead, he calmly knelt down and prayed. Through his prayers and his trust in the Lord, the storm miraculously subsided and the skies cleared, and then calmed. The lives of everyone aboard were spared, and to this day, St. Nicholas is known also as the protector of sailors and travellers.

"His unwavering faith is an incredible example for everyone," said Elizabeth, as she looked with much admiration upon the man whose commemorative statue stood in the centre of the garden. She added, "This truly is a wonderful man."

"And still, dear child, there is more that you must learn about him." The gentle man looked at her with a glimmer in his eye, while Elizabeth gazed back at him and listened intently, eager to learn more about the wonderful saint.

Before beginning the next story, the man said, "Don't be troubled, girl, by these next stories. For while they may start out ominously, they each end with much joy."

"The first story," the bearded man proceeded, "is about three students who travelled to Athens to study. Along the way, they were robbed and murdered by an innkeeper, who hid their remains in a large tub. St. Nicholas followed along the same route shortly after, and stayed in the same inn. While he slept, he dreamt of the evil deeds performed by the innkeeper. He immediately awoke and called upon the wicked man, who showed him where he hid the students. With much faith, St. Nicholas prayed that God would restore the children to life and return them to their families. Indeed, God answered these prayers of St. Nicholas."

"It is so wonderful of him to look after and care for children, and to have so much faith," said Elizabeth, now looking upon the statue with a big smile that showed much thanks upon her face.

"Even *after* his death," continued the gentle, bearded man, "St. Nicholas was known to help children. Hundreds of years ago, the folks here in Myra were celebrating the feast of St. Nicholas, which occurs on December 6th. Pirates came through the town that day and stole treasures from the Church of St. Nicholas, and then snatched a young boy as they left, intending for him to be their slave. For the next year, the boy was made to bring wine every day to their king; the wine was carried in a shiny golden cup. As December 6th arrived the following year, the mother could not take part in the celebration, as she regarded it as a day of tragedy because of the loss of her son. However, she did hold a quiet observance in her home, praying for the life of her son, and for his safekeeping. On that very day, as the boy was about to serve the wine to the king, the spirit of St. Nicholas appeared, and blessed the boy. He then whisked the boy away, to return him to his home in Myra. Much joy and celebration occurred, as the boy appeared, holding the golden cup, with his parents still kneeling in prayer. This story, and others like it, have given St. Nicholas the primary identity of a protector of children."

Elizabeth was touched by the stories that the bearded

man had told, and said, "This St. Nicholas truly *was* a saint; his heart was pure, and he was a very caring man."

"You are right, dear girl," the man replied, "but there is even more, beyond these stories. When St. Nicholas was a young boy, his wealthy parents taught him to be a devoted Christian, dedicated to the teachings of Jesus, and he eventually grew up to be a priest, and then the Bishop of Myra. But while he was still very young, his wealthy parents died. Because of what they taught him, though, Nicholas used the entire inheritance that was left behind for him to help those in need, including the sick and the suffering, the poor, and of course, children. Many of his acts of kindness and generosity were done in secret, as he expected nothing in return. His unconditional love and generosity made Nicholas a true friend of Jesus, and a true follower of the teachings of Jesus." With these words, the man had finished his story.

Having nearly forgotten the reason for her sadness, it was with just a small sniffle that Elizabeth said, "Kind sir, I thank you for these heartwarming stories, and for telling me of this wonderful man. But why do you share these with me?"

"Elizabeth," he started, "I know that you have some doubts, some uncertainties, and some questions in your heart, about what to believe at Christmas."

Elizabeth was surprised, and replied, "How could you know these things about me? I just met you, and I never told you – ."

With a smile, the man raised his hand and reminded the girl, "Remember, Elizabeth, since you are a child of God, I know who you are. Therefore, I also know what you feel, and what you think."

Elizabeth was content and reassured by his answer, and his honesty. And so, he continued, "You wonder why your parents raised you to believe in Santa Claus, and whether their stories are true, or whether the ideas of the students at school are true. You cling to the joy of believing in him, and yet, you wonder what to believe in case it may somehow be possible that Santa does not exist."

Elizabeth now stared earnestly into the glimmering eyes of the man beside her. She hoped that somehow he would be able to give an answer that would comfort her and take away the worries and doubts in her heart. After a short pause, Elizabeth nodded, indicating that the man was right with everything he had just said and, with her eyes, she begged him to continue with his response.

"Elizabeth," he continued, "I promise you, St. Nicholas *did* live, and he brought help and love to all of those who needed it the most, because he chose to follow the teachings of Jesus. There truly is a holiday that celebrates this man, and it pays tribute to his generosity and compassion. Indeed, there are churches and statues throughout the world that are dedicated to him, and to the many wonders that he performed while he was alive.

"Now, others in the world wanted to be able to tell the story of such a generous man. And so, the spirit of St. Nicholas became known as Santa Claus in certain parts of the world. Santa is also a generous man, bringing joy to children of the world by leaving a toy for them every year on Christmas Eve. Through the continuing stories of St. Nicholas and of Santa Claus, we learn of how happy it can feel to bring love, happiness, and gifts to others. This is why your parents have taught you the many stories of Santa Claus.

"With Santa Claus, however, we are not sure if anyone has actually ever seen this jolly man. There is little *proof* about him, about where he lives, or all of the wonderful stories of how he travels, what he does throughout the year, and his workshop. It is those people in the world that need proof that things exist *before* they will believe in them, that unfortunately bring doubts and confusion to those who want to believe. To all of those who don't believe, or who struggle with belief, I say this – look back to the days of your younger youth, when joy, faith, and unwavering belief filled your heart with wonder and complete trust. Remember those marvelous nights in December, when magic and miracles and fascination filled your hearts and minds with tales of generosity at Christmas. How wonderful it was - and is - to have faith, and belief – without question! What others think, of what we feel in our hearts to be true, is of no matter."

The man paused, so that Elizabeth might comprehend all that he was saying, and then added, "Elizabeth, let your heart be light and filled with joy. Just because something or someone is not seen does not mean that it does not exist. I know in your heart that you believe in Jesus. Truly, your concern for orphaned children, for children without hope, for children in poverty who may not receive a wrapped gift on Christmas shows that you are indeed a child of God. We are told that it has been 2000 years since Jesus walked the earth, and performed his many wonders and miracles. And yet, have any of us alive today ever seen him in person? Still, we believe. We see Jesus in the smile of a child, in the laughter of our friends, in the love of our parents and families, in the beauty of the world, in the glory of a sunset, in all acts of kindness, generosity, and compassion, no matter how small.

"Elizabeth, fear not what gifts the unfortunate will

receive at Christmas. For *all* of us throughout the world, whether young or old, rich or poor, sick or healthy, happy or sad, will receive the greatest gift possible – eternal salvation, in the form of an infant boy, wrapped in swaddling clothes. This gift will bring hope for all. It will bring peace, joy, and happiness. And still, none of us alive will actually ever see this gift, or who it comes from."

Elizabeth's eyes brightened and widened with that very sentence. It was simple, but it was true! The gift that *everyone* around the world receives every year, is indeed the best present and act of generosity that we could *all* receive. The Baby Jesus, she thought, brings so much joy and love to the world, and yet, we never question who he comes from, or if the gift-giver is real or not. We just believe! And how the giver of this gift must truly love us, to give us such a precious present, *every* Christmas!

Elizabeth then thought of how St. Nicholas modelled his life after the teachings of Jesus, bringing much help and generosity to the world, even though he never *saw* Jesus. He just believed, and he happily received the wonderful gifts that Jesus gave, and he then shared these with the needy.

Elizabeth continued the thought – If Santa Claus is a modified image of St. Nicholas, bringing joy and hope in the form of gifts to children throughout the world, then it *is* okay and right for me to believe in the spirit of generosity and kindness that *is* Santa Claus! I don't need to see him in order to believe, she thought. And I don't need others to tell me if he is real or not. I know what is right in my heart. I know what gives me hope and joy if I believe in it – I believe in the wrapped infant Jesus that I receive every year. I believe in the incredible generosity and compassion of St. Nicholas, gift-giver and patron saint of children and of sailors and travellers. So yes, I believe in the wonder, the fascination, and the joy that is Santa Claus at Christmas!

The man with the thick wavy beard smiled as he sat beside Elizabeth. He knew that his stories of St. Nicholas, and of Jesus, and of Santa Claus, had reached her. He recognized the magic and the sparkle in her eyes that he had seen in all of her previous Christmases. He was now certain that he would see that same glimmer of hope and enchantment in her eyes for all of her Christmases still to come.

With a bright smile, and a heart full of happiness, Elizabeth hugged the man beside her, on the bench in front of the stone statue, and then woke up....

It was Christmas Eve. Elizabeth spent the day as she always had – of course with her family, but also with much joy and anticipation. The words of the Grade 5 and 6 students would not discourage her. Instead, she knew that she was going to receive special gifts tomorrow – gifts of love, of peace, of compassion, of generosity. The most special of these would be the gift of salvation.

Elizabeth knew that she may not see the givers of any of these gifts on Christmas morning. But because of what she learned from the bearded man in her dream – of St. Nicholas and of Jesus – she would always believe in the wonder and generosity of Santa Claus. It was a gift that she passed on to everyone that she met and loved, and to those that needed to hear it the most, for as long as she lived.

MOST WONDROUS GIFT

Lights of colour beautify the church this holy night;
Poinsettias round the altar with their petals, soft and bright.
Everlasting evergreens adorn the sanctuary,
Between the wooden Joseph and the Blessed Mother, Mary.

In front of them is resting the divine nativity;
A simple grotto shelters Heaven's Holy Family.
The animals surround them and the shepherds gaze, in awe,
As Baby Jesus smiles, from the manger filled with straw.

Our friends and families fill the pews to almost overflowing -
We're comforted with warmth, while out the window, it is snowing.
We carol songs that fill our souls with peace and mild revere,
And pray that we can keep it close throughout the coming year.

It's Christmas Eve – the essence of this holy night surrounds!
Our church is filled with love and peace, and gentle, joyful sounds.
And yet, against the trimming that adorns the church this eve,
Is, set in opposition, the salvation we received.

For in the wooden manger, with a smile upon His face,
Our Saviour's arms are stretching for the world to embrace;
But set behind the altar, on a crucifix, so bare,
His arms are stretched upon a cross, with Christmas everywhere.

Amidst the beauty of the church we've gathered in this night,
We can't forget: He came to die – our Saviour's willful plight.
His death for us on Calvary – most brutal crucifixion –
Gave us salvation with His most triumphant resurrection!

And so, we celebrate His birth this peaceful eventide,
Remembering: our souls were saved when He was crucified.
We thank Him for eternal life – most wondrous gift received,
By gathering to praise His birth on every Christmas Eve.

THE RINGER OF THE BELLS

Joseph was a happy boy. Growing up in a country village that was embraced by the rolling hills of Pleasant Valley, Joseph was surrounded by the friendly animals and the natural wonders of the outdoors, which he loved dearly, and he had the close friendships of his many school friends and the warmhearted relations of his friendly neighbours. All of this made his life as a young boy a wonderful thing, indeed!

The focus of Joseph's happiness, though, came from his family. He had loving parents who worked hard and cared for him deeply, and shared in his every joy; they would do anything to ensure his happiness, health and safety. His mother, Catherine, walked him every day to the one-room schoolhouse beside their church, near the centre of town. She made breads and pastries for the village bakery, and she loved Joseph dearly, thanking God daily for her role as his mother. His father, Jonah, was a woodsman who learned woodcraft from his own father. He had helped to build several of the village buildings, but he saved his finer work for the pews, the altar, the cross, and the interior construction of the village church, where he spent Sundays volunteering as an adult server.

Much of the content that Joseph received from his family came from his younger brother, Benjamin. At four years of age, the young boy followed Joseph everywhere, hanging onto his every word, and looking up to Joseph with much admiration. Joseph and Benjamin shared a room together, and their dog Max was given turns sleeping at the ends of their beds. The boys were inseparable, and along with faithful Max, the three were constant companions who were often seen playing or running together along the dirt road in front of their home and into the flowery fields of Pleasant Valley. Together with Max, the boys would frolic throughout late spring evenings, lazy days of summer, and into the cooler autumn afternoons, sharing undying brotherly love and creating wonderful lifelong memories. Into the winter, they would toboggan on the hills of the valley and Joseph would show Benjamin how to build snowmen and snow angels in their yard. It was obvious to everyone that Joseph's family was the main source of his happiness.

Joseph also found pleasure from the warmth of the small country church in his little village. Together with his family, he spent every Sunday morning and every special religious celebration in the wooden pews of the cozy chapel. It was there that he saw all of his friends and the familiar faces of the friendly townspeople. Along with Benjamin and his mother, he would sit on the left side of two rows of pews, at the front of the church. There was usually room for two or three others on the bench, and there were fourteen more benches behind him. Along the sides of the church were exquisite stained-glass windows depicting the Stations of the Cross, and the entry was large, so that everyone could gather following the mass.

The priest and a server would walk out from the small sacristy onto the sanctuary, dressed in their flowing cassocks, and approach the altar, where they presented the mass in front of the entire congregation. For as long as he could remember, Joseph's father had been the main altar server in their little church. He watched intently when his father would light the altar candles before the start of each mass, and then carry the cross out towards the altar at the beginning of the service. Later, Joseph's father would assist in the washing and rinsing of the priest's hands during the offertory, and then hold the shiny golden communion plate when helping with the serving of communion. Joseph greatly respected his father for these roles he performed as an altar server.

To Joseph, however, the most esteeming part of the whole service was during the offertory, when the priest presented the body, and then the blood of Christ, to the entire congregation. Each time, Joseph's father would reach down behind the altar and gently shake a handle that held three golden bells that rang throughout the church. For those brief moments, the ringing of the bells coinciding with Jesus' gifts of his body and blood signified the most honourable moment of the mass, especially to Joseph. For this, he always thought of his father as the 'Ringer of the Bells', and it was a job that he hoped to someday fulfill.

Out of all of the church services throughout the year, Joseph's favourite mass was on Christmas Eve. He always arrived early with his family to help decorate the church. Flowing garlands were hung in the entrance, and natural wreaths were placed on the end of each pew. A large felt banner was hung on the wall behind the altar that depicted shepherds on the hills on their way to the stable that housed the Holy Family. Three real Christmas trees were set up near the altar, with just a few simple strands of tinsel, and a nativity set was placed in front of the altar, with the Holy Family, and several shepherds and animals. Outside in front of the church, a simple crèche was set up near the entrance that displayed Jesus in his straw manger, along with Joseph and Mary. "It was a very simple birth," Catherine would say, adding, "so we shall keep our decorations simple, but beautiful." And indeed they were.

Every year, as Joseph remembered, the townspeople would arrive early on Christmas Eve – a full hour before midnight – and gather in song before the start of the service. The building would be completely filled, and extra benches were often set up along the side walls, underneath the stained glass windows, to accommodate visitors and the large congregation. The entire village would gather in the little church and fill it with a comfortable coziness that would not be felt at any other time throughout the year. Joseph often suspected that the sound of the music and singing must have echoed through the hills of Pleasant Valley for many miles into the stillness of Christmas Eve.

While Joseph had certainly revered his father's special role as Ringer of the Bells at regular masses throughout the year, he most honoured this role on Christmas Eve. The whole town would gather, clustered together in the pretty little village church; yet the entire congregation would be completely silent during the ringing of the bells at offertory. And on that one night – on Christmas Eve - there was an extra ringing of the bells when one of the village children would carry the infant Christ child from the back of the church to the altar, to be placed in his cradle in the nativity. Throughout that entire entrance, the bells would be ringing softly. Joseph imagined how honourable it would feel to be the altar server who rang the bells on Christmas Eve, signifying Jesus' birth and welcoming his wonderful arrival. Truly, Christmas was a special time for the young boy, and he cherished it deeply.

As he started Grade 4 that year, Joseph received a surprise from his father, who said, "Joseph, Father Daniel has asked if I would like to have an assistant altar server. I can think of no one I'd rather have with me beside the altar than you. Would you like to be my assistant?"

An overwhelming tingling sensation swept over Joseph because of the surprise of the question he just heard. He pictured himself helping out his father on the altar, and he even dared to imagine being the Christmas Eve Ringer of the Bells, before blurting out, "Of course, Father! I would love to be your assistant altar server! I will practice every day after school, and I will make Father Daniel very proud of me. Oh, thank-you, Father. I will be a great altar boy!"

Joseph kept his promise. Every day after school, he visited with Father Daniel and practiced his role as an altar boy. He soon performed his various duties flawlessly, having observed his father's motions and roles for as long as he could remember. He was even permitted during practices to sometimes handle the bells, and to see how it felt to ring them, and to hear their melodious ringing bounce off the walls within the church. This was always an incredible moment for Joseph –

the chance to at least *practice* being the Ringer of the Bells.

Every Sunday, he stood proudly with his father at the side of the altar, and he was often given new roles to perform. One week he was the 'Carrier of the Cross' during the entrance onto the altar. Another week he was the 'Lighter of the Candles'. Before long, Joseph assisted with the offertory, bringing the wine and water for Father Daniel to mix, and a small white cloth that Father Daniel could use afterwards to wipe his hands. Joseph was becoming an essential part of the mass each week, and he was proud of his special contributions. Even Benjamin often praised his older brother, saying, "Joseph, you are a very good altar boy. Jesus will be very happy and proud of you!"

Joseph continued with his varying assistant-altar-server roles well into the fall, and with his many friends, his loving family, his life at school, and his faithful dog Max, he was living a very full and blessed life. He truly was a happy boy.

All of this changed on a snowy day in December. Joseph was sitting on his chair in the one-room schoolhouse, on the last day of classes before Christmas. A knock could be heard from the side entrance, and only a moment after answering the door, Joseph's teacher immediately summoned him towards her.

"Joseph," she spoke, "you must put your coat, boots, and mitts on right now, and go outside. Your mother is waiting for you."

Joseph quickly had his winter wear on, and he rushed out the doorway. From the top of the steps just outside the school entrance, he could see a tear glistening on his mother's rosy face. He scrunched his brows in confusion, and then ran to meet with his mother. As he reached her, he grabbed her hands and asked, "What is it, Mother," though he was worried to hear her response.

"Oh Joseph," she sobbed, "we must go quickly!"

"What, Mother? What has happened," he continued. Joseph had never seen such a look of worry and concern on his mother's face.

"It's Benjamin," she replied. "He's sick. He has pneumonia, and the doctor is unsure if he'll recover."

Joseph learned of the sickness at school, and how even a few residents of Pleasant Valley had succumbed to the disease over the years. Benjamin *had* developed a cough over the last few days; but he was getting his rest, and his sickness didn't seem to worsen. When Doctor Lucas visited, he concluded that it was just a cold that Benjamin picked up from a virus that was going around the village. The doctor advised that Benjamin remain indoors, where he had been treated to warm soups and cocoa, and tucked into bed early during the last few nights. It seemed routine, but from the urgency in his mother's voice, Joseph knew that it had now become much worse. He ran with his mother down the street to his home, bursting through the front doors upon his arrival.

From inside the porch, he could see the doctor's leather medical bag on the floor beside Benjamin's bed. Max, ever a part of the family, lay curled in a corner beside the bed, and Joseph's father was inside from his workshop, kneeling to lean over his youngest son. Benjamin was shaking, and his cheeks were moist from tears.

"I'm here, Benjamin," Joseph said, bringing a brief smile to the youngest boy's face.

"What…what's wrong, Doctor Lucas," Joseph asked.

"I'm afraid it's serious, Joseph. Your brother's cough is much worse, and he now has a high fever, and pains in his chest. And he shakes with chills, even with these warm blankets over him. It's all happened so quickly. Overnight. I've seen this before, Joseph, and I know how serious it has become for Benjamin. I don't want any of you to risk too much getting sick yourselves, so I don't want you to spend too much time too close to him. Joseph, you will have to sleep somewhere else tonight. But *do* spend time near Benjamin. He needs your comfort, and your love. I've treated him, and have done what I can; he now needs plenty of rest. But the disease has grabbed hold of him so strong, and so fast. I will stay, but I'm afraid that the best any of us can do now is pray."

"Benjamin," Joseph said, "I love you, my little brother. You are my best friend, and I am so sad to see you like this. We are all sad. There's new snow outside, and I want to pull you and Max on our toboggan, and play with you on the valley hills, and make snowmen, and snow angels, just like before. And tomorrow is Christmas Eve! We have the glory and the music of our midnight mass to attend, and we have the Baby Jesus to welcome. It could never be as special without you. But the doctor is right," Joseph continued, "there is one thing we *can* do. We can pray. We will be with you, Benjamin, and we will pray."

"Father," Joseph added, "can Father Daniel come and help us pray?"

"Of course," his father said. "Why don't you come with me, and we will ask Father to join us?"

"We will be back very soon, Benjamin," Joseph told his brother. "Doctor Lucas, Mother and Max will wait with you, and when we return, we will all pray, together."

Joseph and his father were quickly on their way, hurrying down the street, and they soon arrived knocking at the door of the church. When Father Daniel answered, they explained everything to him. Father Daniel put on his overcoat and boots and returned with Joseph and his father. Along the way, he added, "Joseph, I know you are ready for the Christmas Eve service tomorrow night. I will pray with you, and your family, and if we can be blessed with a miracle, there is a special assignment that I will ask of you, when the moment is right. But for now, let us go to be with your brother, and let us ask the Lord to be with us, as we pray."

Together, Joseph, his parents, Doctor Lucas and Father Daniel surrounded Benjamin as he lay on his bed in the dimly lit room. They prayed the Our Father, and then Father Daniel led them in praying the rosary. They then took turns thanking God for the blessings they had despite the turmoil they were going through, and for blessing them with Benjamin, who brought joy to their lives every day. It was the day before Christmas Eve, and Benjamin appeared very ill before them; but the family knelt around Joseph's brother and held their hands in prayer.

Joseph looked up to his mother and father, and said, "We must have hope. Without hope, there is little to look forward to, and I know that Jesus wants us to look forward to our lives, and to live them as best as we can. We are a family. Let us pray and hope as a family that Jesus will come this Christmas with a blessing for all of us."

Benjamin was at last resting in sleep. With everyone gathered around him in prayer, he slept through the rest of the day. By nighttime, his fever had peaked, and remained steady, and Doctor Lucas and Father Daniel returned home. Benjamin's mother remained on a rocking chair beside him through the night, holding a rosary and a picture of her baby boy. His father remained too, bringing comfort to his wife and further prayers for his son. And of course, Max remained curled on the floor in the corner beside the bed.

As expected, Joseph preferred to stay in their room, too, so that he could sleep near his brother and watch over him. But his parents advised, "Joseph, you have done everything that you could have, and everything that Jesus would have wanted you to do. But you need your sleep, and you need to be healthy. Keep Benjamin in your heart tonight, and keep praying for a miracle, so that maybe he will be with us to join in the wonder of Christmas Eve."

Joseph's parents set up a bed of blankets for him on the floor in the common room, close to the fireplace and their wonderfully decorated tree. They tucked Joseph in, and then said a little prayer with him, asking for Benjamin's returning health.

Joseph lay on his side near the pretty nativity beneath their tree. He leaned towards it, gazing upon the Baby Jesus in the crib, and then whispered, "Dear Jesus, I know that, on Christmas morning, you will come to be with us. You will bring us the most marvelous gift of hope, and the promise of an eternal life with you. This is such a wonderful gift!" Joseph then added, "But please, Jesus, can you come to us a day early, here in Pleasant Valley, and can you please help my brother Benjamin to recover from his illness? He has brought so much joy and fun to my life. Without him, I will be very sad. Can you *please* help us, dear Lord? Amen."

While Joseph's mind was filled with worry, his heart was filled with hope, and faith, and he was blessed with a much needed, restful sleep.

Benjamin's mother and father sat with him through the night, praying for their little boy, remembering Joseph's words that they must keep hope. They took turns resting, and at times were fortunate enough to enter sleep.

As the midnight hours crawled along, a little miracle seemed to unfold in the hopeful family's humble home in Pleasant Valley. As 11:00 became 12:00, and then 1:00, and then 2:00, Benjamin's cough subsided, and eventually stopped, and his breathing became deep, and clear. And along with it, Benjamin's fever also cleared, so that by 4:00, his temperature had returned to normal. Benjamin was sleeping restfully, and still, and the illness that seized his body only a few hours ago seemed to have vanished as quickly as it had come!

Jonah and Catherine became overwhelmed with hope, and they embraced each other, in tears. Soon after, Jonah was dressed in his winter clothes, and was hurrying out the door beneath the dark, starry sky of Christmas Eve morning. Moments later, he had returned with Doctor Lucas and Father Daniel, having shared his news with them, and they were removing their boots to hurry to the boys' bedroom, careful not to waken Joseph as they shuffled by him. Doctor Lucas checked Benjamin's chest, and his breathing, and administered a thorough check-up, while Father Daniel began a rosary. Doctor Lucas confirmed that the fluid in Benjamin's lungs had disappeared, and that he was breathing normally, and rhythmically. Benjamin's fever was also gone, as his temperature had returned to normal, and his skin was dry, as his chills had vanished.

The morning of Christmas Eve crept over the hills, bringing a glorious sunrise throughout Pleasant Valley and into the boys' bedroom. Benjamin awoke, alert, to see his parents, Doctor Lucas and Father Daniel standing over him, holding hands and sharing a look of overwhelming hope, and joy. On his bed, Max sat beside him, wagging his tail and panting.

Benjamin's mother spoke to him, "Good morning my son! How are you feeling on this Christmas Eve?"

"Mother! Father! It is Christmas Eve? What a beautiful day it is," he replied, noticing the sun's rays glistening off the snow around the edges of his window, adding, "I feel perfect! How else could I feel on this wonderful day?"

Tears of joy streamed down the faces of everyone standing in the room. They had all witnessed a wonderful gift from Heaven - a miracle that saved the life of a little boy on the morning of Christmas Eve.

Benjamin saw Joseph's empty bed and asked, "Where is my brother on this beautiful day?"

"He is still asleep beside the fireplace," Jonah replied. "He prayed *so* much for you, Benjamin. He loves his little brother dearly, and he never lost hope or faith that, somehow, a miracle would bless us this Christmas. Why don't you go see if he's awake?"

Benjamin looked at Doctor Lucas and Father Daniel, who both nodded in approval. Jonah and Catherine first hugged their little boy, and then watched as he tiptoed towards his sleeping brother. Benjamin knelt down, and gently shook Joseph's shoulder. Joseph's eyes opened, and as he recovered from his drowsiness, his face lit up in shock and surprise.

"Benjamin! Is it really you," he asked, with just a hint of disbelief that was otherwise overpowered by hope.

"Of course, my big brother! I am here. I am well," he said. "And today is Christmas Eve. There is sunshine everywhere, and lots of fresh snow. Let us go toboggan on the hills, and make snowmen, and snow angels, just like before!"

"Oh, my little brother," Joseph said. "Jesus is coming twice this Christmas! I prayed for him to come last night, and he did. You are here, and well. And of course," Joseph continued, "Jesus will come tomorrow morning and bring us the most glorious day of all! Yes, Benjamin! Let's play! Let's celebrate!" On their way outside, Joseph stopped by the little nativity underneath their Christmas tree, and leaned in towards it, whispering, "Thank you, Jesus!"

Doctor Lucas and Father Daniel stayed for a cup of tea and a Danish before leaving. Doctor Lucas was thanked for his medical guidance during the crisis, and Father Daniel was thanked for his spiritual support, and for his prayers and support. As they left, Father Daniel said to Jonah and Catherine, "I'd like to ask a favour of you, regarding Benjamin. Do you think he would like to carry the infant Jesus up to the altar at tonight's service?"

"Of course, he'd be delighted," they immediately replied, adding, "We are honoured that you asked us, Father!"

"One thing, though," Father Daniel continued, "please don't tell Joseph. I want it to be a surprise for him. And if I can ask one more favour – is it okay if I ask Joseph to be my main server at tonight's service?'

"Oh, Father," they replied, "he will be so thrilled! Yes, yes, Joseph can be your server. We will tell him when the boys return." With that, Father Daniel departed to prepare for midnight mass.

Joseph and Benjamin played all afternoon, and their faithful friend Max was with them in all of their play. They tobogganed on the hills of Pleasant Valley, and they made snowmen, and then snow angels, in the freshly fallen snow in front of their home. Max skipped and playfully yelped beside them the whole time.

Evening arrived, and after supper, the family gathered to sing carols beside their tree. Jonah read The Christmas Story to his boys, while they were treated to fresh hot cross buns and pastries that Catherine lovingly prepared throughout the afternoon. The aromas, the decorations, the music and the togetherness filled their home with true Christmas sentiment.

By 10:30, the family dressed in their formal wear to prepare for midnight mass. Benjamin and Joseph both wore black pants with red shirts and black ties, and Catherine styled their hair just right. Benjamin was told of the favour that Father Daniel had asked of him, and he quickly agreed. Joseph was then approached with Father Daniel's second requested favour, "Joseph, while you were outside playing, Father left a message for you that we think you will enjoy hearing. He wants you to be the main server at midnight mass."

Joseph's jaw nearly dropped as he stood before his parents with a look of wonder on his face. "The Ringer of the Bells," he thought. "Everyone will be waiting in silence for the sound of the bells tonight, and I will be the one to ring them!"

"Yes, Father and Mother, of *course* I will be Father's main server. I am so honoured; I will do a wonderful job....if that's all right with you, Father."

Jonah smiled at his son, and said, "Of course, Joseph. I am so proud of you! Father is giving you such a wonderful gift for Christmas, and I know that you are the best person to receive it!" Jonah then said to all of his family, "Come everyone, let us go celebrate the birth of Jesus!"

The congregation gathered early, as usual, and all of their favourite hymns were beautifully sung before the start of mass. At precisely 12:00, Father Daniel, Joseph and then Jonah entered onto the sanctuary. Joseph led them, carrying the cross, and he placed it in its holder beside the pulpit, next to three evergreen trees. He then stood with his hands pressed together in front of his chest, at one side of the altar.

Father Daniel stood behind the altar, with Jonah on his left and Joseph on his right, and he led the congregation in a brief prayer to open the midnight mass.

Now, it was time for the procession of the Christ Child, so Jonah, Joseph and the entire assembly knelt in adoration. Joseph looked up at his father and smiled, and then he looked out at all of the gathered townspeople, who were watching him, and waiting. Then Joseph gazed at his mother, expecting also to see Benjamin; but he wasn't there. Instead, as Joseph looked behind the congregation, he saw his little brother standing alone in the entrance, holding the little Jesus figurine, and wearing a special green gown over his clothes.

Joseph stared in amazement, and then he reached down and began gently ringing the little golden bells. He looked back up and sent a wide, happy smile to his brother, as Benjamin began to walk forward with the infant child. The entire crowd waited silently, watching as Benjamin walked along the centre aisle, and listening to Joseph's gentle ringing of the bells. Joseph smiled at the Christ Child as Benjamin brought him forth, cradling him in his arms. One incredible miracle had already come to Pleasant Valley this Christmas, and now, before the entire congregation, a second one had arrived. "Happy birthday, Jesus," Joseph whispered, before adding, "and Merry Christmas!"

A joyful tear escaped from Joseph's eye, as he realized his dream of being the Ringer of the Bells. His faith and hope brought him two truly wonderful gifts this Christmas, and while he would have no other Christmas quite like it, he joyfully shared the rest of his childhood Christmases with Benjamin. Indeed, Joseph was a happy boy!

CHRISTMAS IN THE VALE

The moon hovers brightly in a clear, cool sky,

Spreading a luminous glow over the snow-capped hills,

Across their evergreens, and throughout the valley,

All below a December night sky that has tinted the entire scene

with a purplish hue;

And on this peaceable Eve,

A once-a-year scene has begun to unfurl.

The charming vale is hushed in serenity,
And even the stream at the foot of the hills is asleep,
Bathed in a beam of moonlight which envelops the forest
And the beings within.

A dusting of snow hugs the lustrous limbs of evergreens,
And in the light of a glorious star,
Their shimmering needles reflect a lovely emerald gleam,
A wonderful sparkling that dances among the green of the boughs
in this Christmassy dream!

So soft, so gentle is the downy cover of snow
That conceals the ground between the stream and the trees;
Velvety smooth, it's a delicate drape that flashes with a trillion
twinkling lights as it wraps the vale in silence.

A wispy twirl of smoke escapes from the chimney of a lone, but
cozy, country cottage;
Its peaked roof is warmed by a blanket of snow,
While bright red ribbons and flowing green garland adorn its
wooden veranda.

A glow from the lights within bursts through every window
To paint a golden highlight that dances on the twinkling snow,
Stretching to a short finger of land that reaches into
The crystal-clear waters of the silent stream.

And there, to welcome this night – behold...a wooden crèche!
Lit by the light flowing from the cottage,
The lustre of the moonbeam,
And the shine from the wondrous star,

It is aglow in the near-dark of Christmas Eve!

Its weathered wooden planks form a simple little shelter
Where Joseph stands over his family,
And Mary kneels in front of a crib, cradling her Baby Jesus
As she sings him a Christmas Eve lullaby.

And too, by the shore of the tranquil little stream,
The vale's creatures have come to enjoy the Christmas Eve peace,
Lying in rest beside the Holy Family.
The woodland wonders have gathered there, again,
As with many years before,
To enjoy a night of stillness and peace,
And to welcome a miracle in the silence of the vale.

And so, on the shore of a still, clear stream,
In a countryside of rolling hills and evergreens –
Covered with glistening snow –
A marvelous vale twinkles of green and gold and blue,
Beneath the light of the moon, a brilliant star, and the warm glow
from within a solitary cabin.
Christmas has once again come to this magical scene –
So simply, so quietly, so wonderfully.
And in the morning to come, all the world will rejoice.

UNDER THE TREE

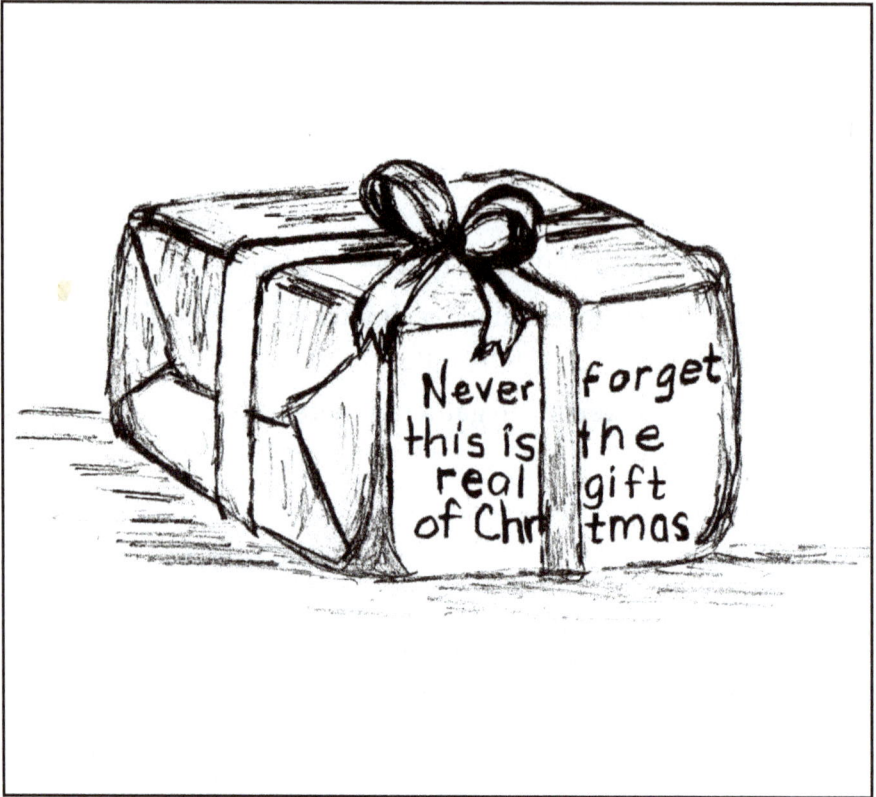

Never forget this is the real gift of Chr[is]tmas

Christmas this year was going to be very hard for Aaron
– that was for certain. Just 8 years old, he had lost his parents in
a tragic accident, leaving him alone and understandably full of
fear and uncertainty as his world had collapsed upon him.
Fortunately, his solitude and worry would be short-lived, for as
he stood with tears on his face, dressed in his best clothes as he
offered his last goodbye to his loving parents, Aaron was
embraced by his aunt, his mother's only sister, who
immediately, happily, and lovingly adopted her orphaned
nephew and welcomed him into her family as one of her own –
a new brother for her own two children.

Aaron's favourite season of Christmas was rapidly

approaching. But without his mother and father, it wouldn't – and couldn't – be the same. He couldn't help but remember and daydream of how wonderful their Christmases were together – filled with love, and family, and celebration of the birth of the Saviour! After Christmas Eve mass, they would return to their little home, gather around a special red candle that they lit only at Christmas, kneel on the floor with their hands joined, and pray the rosary. Then they would give thanks for each of their blessings, sing some of their favourite traditional carols, and exchange a gift before bedtime.

Aaron's favourite gift, and now his only – and most prized – possession, was the gift that he had received just last Christmas. With great detail and precision, his father had carved from wood the characters of the nativity. There was a robed and bearded Joseph, a smiling, kneeling Mary, and the beautiful little Christ child, sleeping in his manger. A shepherd, a cow, a donkey, and three sheep were also part of Aaron's special gift. "Oh Papa, you must have worked so long on the beautiful figures of this nativity. Thank you! Thank you," exclaimed Aaron, as he took turns handling each figure with great care. The nativity set had been wrapped in a beautiful tan-coloured cloth that was tied at the top with a shiny red ribbon. On the cloth, with red thread, Aaron's mother had stitched the words, "Never forget, this is the real gift of Christmas".

As Christmas Eve arrived in his aunt's home, everyone prepared for the evening's mass at the church. Aaron dressed quickly and hurried into the large parlour room at the front of the house. There, Aaron unwrapped his nativity characters and set them carefully under the sprawling lower branches of a massive, wonderfully decorated fir tree, topped with a white glowing angel. The wooden figures were almost hidden underneath the tree, as they were placed right beside the stand, a full three feet from the outer edge of the lower branches. It was the perfect place, as one yellow tree light dangled there loosely from a branch, providing a faint glow that shrouded Aaron's precious wooden nativity characters.

Aaron crawled back out from under the tree, stood back, and gazed lovingly upon the wooden Holy Family. His eyes welled with tears as he remembered how joyful he felt when he unwrapped the gift just one year ago. In the silence and darkness of the parlour room, save the lights on the tree, Aaron whispered, "Dear Mama and Papa, thank you so much for this most wonderful gift. I miss you so much and I am so sad without you; but I know that you are now with Jesus in Heaven. What a wonderful place to be on Christmas Eve! Merry Christmas, Mama and Papa. I love you."

Aaron returned from the parlour room in time to join his adoptive family at Christmas Eve mass. Afterwards, they sang carols, and then each child opened one gift. Aaron was very thankful for the picture he was given. It was taken just last summer of him and his parents in front of their little home, and it was the last photograph ever taken of the three of them together. "Thank you, auntie, I love it," he uttered truthfully, even as it brought a tear rolling down his cheek.

It was now getting late, and the children were ushered off to bed, cautioned that St. Nicholas would be arriving soon. Little Aaron lay in bed with a heavy heart, happy that it was Christmas Eve, but very sad because he would be welcoming Jesus' birth without his parents. Aaron clutched the tan cloth that was the wrapping for his nativity set, and held it close to his heart. With a few more hidden tears, Aaron fell asleep on Christmas Eve.

Christmas morning arrived with a burst, as Aaron's stepbrothers ran into his room and shouted, "Get up! Get up! St. Nicholas has come! Jesus is born! Let's open our presents!"

Aaron put on his slippers and housecoat and arrived in the parlour just as his aunt and uncle stepped into the room. The other boys were already picking through the presents, finding the ones with their respective names on them, but Aaron sat quietly and watched with reservation, still clutching the tan cloth wrapping of his nativity figures.

Gifts were opened in turn, and Aaron waited patiently for his aunt to hand him beautifully wrapped presents, which turned out to be a toy Noah's Ark set, a soccer ball, a toy race car track, a model airplane, a frame for the picture of Aaron and his parents, and many various articles of clothing. He had never received such a bounty of gifts before on Christmas morning, and he opened each one of them with more than just a little bit of embarrassment.

Aaron watched as his new brothers almost frantically ripped open their gifts with shrieks of joy. The stack of toys and opened gifts grew larger in front of them, and the parlour floor began to overflow with opened gifts, wrapping, and ribbons, until finally, the last present had been opened. Aaron's aunt called everyone to the centre of the parlour, where hugs and thank-you's were exchanged. She then said, "This has been a very special Christmas. We are grateful to have you here to share it with us, Aaron, and to share many more with us in the years to come. Now, who wants to come to the kitchen for fresh baked buns, hot chocolate, and a Christmas orange?"

Aaron's uncle and brothers wholeheartedly accepted the invitation, and were beginning to exit the parlour, when he unravelled the tan cloth and re-read the words to himself that had been lovingly stitched by his mother – "Never forget, this is the real gift of Christmas". Aaron shyly replied to his aunt's invitation by saying, "But....please wait. There's still another gift under the tree. It's the most important gift of Christmas." Everyone turned and looked back into the parlour, as Aaron continued, "Come. Come. Come and see what has been given to us this morning."

Aaron led his new family towards the tree, moving presents aside so that they could make their way towards the lower branches. "There. Under the tree, next to the stand," he said, gesturing towards his precious wooden figures. Aaron's aunt and uncle had to kneel onto the floor to see under the tree, but at the same time with their children, they noticed the characters of the nativity, next to the tree stand. Seeing that the others had noticed his carefully placed nativity scene, Aaron said to them, "The Baby Jesus resting in the manger. He is the gift still under the tree – the most precious gift of Christmas."

The five of them were kneeling together at the bottom of the tree. Aaron grabbed his aunt's hand, and soon they all held hands in front of the nativity characters. Breaking the moment of silence, Aaron humbly and softly sang, "Happy birthday to you! Happy birthday to you! Happy birthday, dear Jesus! Happy birthday to you!"

Aaron's aunt then led the group in singing two of her favourite Christmas carols. They all knew the words, and rejoiced together as they sang "Hark! The Herald Angels Sing!", followed by "Joy to the World". As they finished the latter song, Aaron's aunt, still kneeling on the floor, looked at him with much love and gratitude, saying, "Oh, thank you, Aaron. Thank you for reminding us of the world's most precious Christmas gift. Of course, you are right – the Baby Jesus came as a saviour for all, and there is no better gift than this!"

Aaron's aunt arose and motioned everyone into the kitchen. Aaron stayed kneeling for a moment, smiling as he looked down again at the words his mother had stitched on the cloth, and the beautiful wooden figures his father had carved for him. He knew that he would never spend another Christmas with his mother and father; but with the special gifts that they lovingly created for him, he knew that they would always be with him. Reflecting on this, Aaron looked at the Baby Jesus and whispered, "Thank you." He added, "Merry Christmas, Jesus," before he arose to join the others for hot chocolate.

A GIFT FROM MANOLO

Six months were quickly drawing to a close. It seemed like just yesterday that Andrew had filled his backpack and boarded the plane bound for Guatemala. Seeking change and something more meaningful in his life, Andrew had signed up to work with kids and put his carpentry skills to use in a little village outside of Antigua. During his stay, he helped to build a new roof on the school, three new homes for the village families, and ten new pews for their little church. He worked with kids at the school, helping them with their courses and teaching them English, and coaching them in soccer three days a week. Two other days during the week and on every weekend, he joined a few other adults in the village to lead a group of children between the ages of 5 and 12 on hikes into the forest, or towards volcano streams and pools where they always stopped to swim and play and refresh themselves from the humidity of the jungle.

Andrew had become very close with the villagers, especially the children, and little Manolo, just six years old, had become his favourite. Manolo always wore a bright, wide smile, and he was a happy and playful child. He had a gentle spirit and was loved by all of the villagers. One day, while enjoying a hike with several of the villagers, Andrew learned from Manolo's father that the boy's name meant Emmanuel - God with us. As Andrew got to know Manolo and his gentle disposition, he discovered Manolo's parents had given the boy a most suitable name; for every day, in Manolo's caring actions and his loving words, the boy truly and unknowingly lived up to the meaning of his name. Andrew knew that when he departed just before Christmas, he was going to sorely miss everyone in the village, but especially Manolo.

With just days now before he would leave behind these loving, caring people, with whom he had shared the last six months of his life, becoming very fond of them during his stay, Andrew learned that on his final night before leaving, the last day of school before Christmas, an annual celebration was planned for the villagers during which everyone would come together for an evening of carols and festivity. He was told that all would gather along the shoreline just beyond the edge of the forest, where the gently rolling waves would lap softly and rhythmically on the sand near their feet, and at the moment the sun faded into the water, painting a deep orange along the horizon, the villagers would proclaim traditional songs of

Christmas and dance by the growing starlight and the flames of their torches. Andrew was wholeheartedly invited to join in the celebration and share his last night with the village people, and he felt incredibly fortunate to be with them, to share in their joyous celebration.

Andrew began to wonder what he could do for the village children, to bring something different, something special to help make their upcoming Christmas celebration a most memorable one. As he sat on a stool outside the school room, leaning forward with his elbow on his knee while rubbing his beard which had grown long and thick during his stay, Andrew pondered, "There must be something I can add to the celebration - a gift that I can leave for Manolo and all of the children." As he peered through the trees to the warm blue waters of the sea, wondering what he could do, Andrew paused and sat up straight, still stroking the coarse hair of his beard, and he began to smile as he thought of a childhood memory of his own that he could share with the villagers.

"Of course," he mused, "I will pose as St. Nicholas, and sit with each one of them, to listen to their Christmas wishes. I will let each student bring me one wish, and then I will pass the aspirations on to their parents, so that the children's dreams for this Christmas can be fulfilled!"

Andrew imagined the bright smiles and laughter of the children when they opened a present from St. Nicholas - the same bright smiles and laughter that he had grown to love - and he decided that such joy on Christmas morning was the best way that he could help to make this Christmas extra special for the children. He wasted no time preparing his gift.

That night, Andrew met with the parents of his students and explained his idea for the Christmas festival; they were delighted with his idea, and agreed to help. He returned to his hut and created a poster for the children, which he brought the next morning to hang at the front of the classroom. With cut-out letters pasted onto a sheet of parchment, his poster read, "We will have a special guest for our Christmas celebration - St. Nicholas!" He had draped a cloth over the poster to hide the announcement, and once all of the children had arrived and had recited their morning prayer, Andrew walked silently to the front of the room, gently tugged the bottom edge of the cloth, and then pulled it away. After the moment it took to read the poster, the children collectively cheered, "St. Nicholas is coming! St. Nicholas is coming!"

Andrew smiled and shared in the children's elation. With amazement, and just a hint of disbelief, which was no doubt shared by his classmates, little Manolo put up his hand, and when prompted, asked, "Is it true? Is St. Nicholas really going to be at our Christmas celebration?"

"It's true," Andrew replied. "He sent me a letter, Manolo! St. Nicholas will be at our Christmas celebration tomorrow evening!"

Continuing then to the entire class, Andrew added, "But he has so many places to go on Christmas Eve, so many children to visit all over the world. We don't want to overwhelm his reindeer, and we certainly wouldn't want St. Nicholas himself to carry a bag that could cause him to stumble. So I would like each of you to think of one gift that you could ask for from St. Nicholas. Think of a *special* gift; something that you think could help to make your Christmas as happy and as memorable as possible."

Their village was a simple one, without extravagance. Hand-made toys, new clothing, Christmas fruits, treats and desserts topped the lists of all the children and danced in their dreams on the night before the celebration.

The last day of school before the Christmas break dawned, and the classroom was filled with great anticipation and excitement, as the children shared, discussed, and daydreamed about the gifts they hoped to receive from St. Nicholas.

"I'm going to ask for a wooden toy truck," exclaimed one, while another declared, "a basket full of pineapple, bananas, coconuts, mangoes, and even some nuts and cashews that I can share with my family, is what I'll ask of St. Nicholas!"

Then another confided that she would ask for "a tray full of gingerbread cookies that I can decorate on Christmas morning; oh I *love* the smell of gingerbread!" To that, another classmate quickly added, "I'm going to ask for a bowl filled with oranges and candy canes and little chocolates!"

What a day of pure childhood fun, imagination, and hope it was for the students in Andrew's class! Together, they revelled in the excitement that grew and filled their hearts and minds through every minute of the last day of school before the Christmas break.

Meanwhile, the villagers were preparing for the Christmas festival. Streamers of red and green were draped several feet off the ground along a forest path that led from the edge of the village for 150 feet to open onto the shore. Torches were placed along the path and in the sand in the shape of a star, and then finally up and down the beach in both directions from the star, to surround their festival. Tables and chairs were set up for the great feast, and off to the side, down a shorter, separate path that wound some fifty feet into the woods, a large wooden chair with a high back and arm rests was set in a small clearing with four torches at its corners. Along with the children's parents, Andrew had found and chosen this as the spot where he would greet the children as St. Nicholas. Following their early evening festival meal, the children would form a line on the beach and, one at a time, walk along the path to present their wish to St. Nicholas.

By the end of the school day, as the children began their Christmas break and hurried home with great anticipation, everything was set for their annual festival and for the special visit from St. Nicholas.

Andrew sorted his books and prepared notes to leave for his replacement in the new year, and then tidied the room. He took a last look around at the little wooden desks, the chalkboard, the three windows along the back wall, and the lone book shelf at the side of the room. He imagined the faces of the children he had worked with over the past several months, and then slowly sighed before turning out the lights for the last time and leaving to prepare for the festival.

For his role at the gathering that evening, Andrew had borrowed a beige cloth robe from the village priest; it had long loose sleeves and a V-shaped top that drew shut with a small lace. It also had a long brown braided cord that Andrew could use to tie around his waist. He folded the robe and placed it in a cloth bag along with the cord, and left to join the others at the festival feast.

Andrew walked down the path to the beach, and was pleased to see everyone gathered and preparing a wonderful meal. The tables were neatly set and filled with basic dinnerware and glasses. Several red candles were spaced in order, and dishes of all sizes full with food completely filled any open space atop the tables.

The villagers stood side by side and joined hands as the priest led them in prayer. Manolo's father then added, "We would also like to thank you, Lord, for blessing us by bringing Andrew into our lives. He has done so much to help us in our village, with his carpentry skills and his work with the children. Please watch over him and take care of him as he leaves us tomorrow."

Andrew thanked Manolo's father for his gracious words, and then looked down beside the man at his son, who stood with a tear in his eye. Andrew smiled at Manolo, apologetically, and winked at the little boy, hoping that his role as St. Nicholas after the feast would bring a smile back to his face.

Everyone sat then and joined in a festive gathering on the beach - and what a feast it was! Roast pig, fish, lobster, potatoes, vegetables, and fruits and desserts of all sorts were shared by everyone, along with an endless supply of laughter, conversation, tales of past festivals, and of course, memories of their time with Andrew over the past six months. A light, warm breeze blew in off the water beneath a wide, cloudless sky, and Andrew savoured the beautiful setting and his last evening with his new friends, as he looked up and down both sides of the table at each face and remembered special times with each one of them.

After nearly two hours on the beach, the sun approached the horizon, and Andrew nodded across the table at Manolo's father and slipped away to put on the robe and tie it with the cord. He sneaked down the path and assumed his spot on the large wooden chair. Some of the elders stood up and said, "Children! Our guest of honour has arrived and is waiting to see you! Come and line up so that you can offer a wish to St. Nicholas!"

The children jumped up and hurried into a line near the woods. One by one, they entered the forest along the short path and sat with Andrew, sharing their wishes with him.

There was the toy truck, the basket of fruit, the gingerbread cookies, and the bowl of candy canes and chocolate - Andrew recorded each of these and all of the others on a small note pad. After a wish was offered up, Andrew smiled and nodded at each child, and then offered a wink as he placed a finger in front of his mouth and whispered, "Don't tell the others it was me. I have written down your wish and I will take it to St. Nicholas when I leave. You will find what you wished for on Christmas Day!"

At last, showing much patience and the smile he was known for, Manolo began his walk down the path. The sun was already spilling into the horizon, and the shadows of the flames danced playfully in the woods, all the way to Andrew's chair. Manolo reached the back of the chair, walked around to the front, and looked up.

In the flickering shadows of the woods, Manolo gazed at the figure before him. Andrew sat peacefully with his hands at the front of the arm rests, smiling with a closed mouth at Manolo. With his thick brown beard and moustache, his long, wavy brown hair, and the large beige robe that cloaked his entire body, Andrew looked little like the image of St. Nicholas that Manolo had pictured. A tingling wave swept over the little boy as he greeted the man who sat before him.

"Jesus," the child began, "it is you!"

Manolo had planned to ask St. Nicholas for a new shirt, since his favourite shirt had a hole in the sleeve, and he felt so embarrassed wearing it at school. But as he stared at the face of what he thought was Jesus, his wish changed, and he said, "Lord, I can ask for nothing for myself. There are so many in this world who are hungry, sick, and dying. But not me. I am full, healthy, and alive. Jesus, can you please help those who need you most? And thank you, Jesus, for bringing Andrew to us. He did so much for us, and he is our friend. I will miss him so much when he leaves tomorrow. Please watch over him."

As he did with all of the other children, Andrew handed Manolo a candy cane; but he couldn't hide the tears on his face as they glistened in the firelight when he leaned forward and hugged Manolo tightly, saying, "I love you, and I'll miss you, Manolo."

Andrew waited for a moment after Manolo walked away so that he could compose himself, wipe away the tears, and remove and put away the robe. He then gathered with the others on the beach just in time to join in the singing of carols, dancing, and a wonderful evening of celebration that carried out well into the night.

The next morning, Andrew greeted each of the village families and said farewell to them, wishing a Merry Christmas and thanking them for the wonderful memories he would take home of his six months with them. A teary Manolo hugged him, saying, "Thank you, Andrew, for everything. Goodbye, and Merry Christmas."

Andrew hugged the boy in return, saying, "I'm the one to thank you, Manolo. You enabled me to love every minute I spent here. Thank you."

Andrew waved as the taxi drove him away. Soon he was sitting in an airplane, looking out the window as the plane lifted away from the runway. He looked in the direction of the village as his memories of the last half year raced through his mind. He remembered with great detail the last week and especially the festivities of his last night in the village. Andrew had planned to give the children a gift for Christmas by starting a tradition of adding St. Nicholas to their festival. Little did he know, though, that Manolo, the little boy from Guatemala whom Andrew had grown to love because of his smile, innocence, and peaceful spirit, would instead give him the most precious gift he would receive for many Christmases to come.

JOSEF'S SONG

Josef's youth was meager, born in poverty, forlorn;
His father left before his birth (a cold December morn').
Alone, his mother raised him, 'cross the river from Old Town,
With just her love, and scarcely more, save sheets of thistledown.

The famine and the cold had often prompted Josef's searching –
On lengthy strolls, he wandered far with unrelenting urging;
With fate, to the Cathedral he was led, in providence,
To meet a priest who'd change his life and bring great consequence.

A father-son relationship was borne from their convening,
Their dialogues led Josef on a course for greater meaning.
The priest's perception helped discern the boy's most inner passion –
He undertook to tend his love for music, with compassion.

So Father Hiernle guided Josef to an education,
And soon his talents flourished as he lived his true vocation;
In Salzburg's churches Josef sang and played the violin,
So pleased to give his gifts to those who shared the Word within.

The seminary beckoned – to the priesthood he was drawn,
A servant of the Lord, the call he'd duly act upon;
At twenty-three, his priestly life began with ordination,
And Josef started out upon his promised consecration.

A mountain village setting, "What great beauty," Josef mused;
An inspiration filled his soul and left his heart enthused –
An inner creativity emerged inevitably,
Incited by the splendour of the lovely scenery!

The countryside surrounding roused his love for exploration,
And all the while, musically he grew, with acclamation;
But Mariapfarr awakened something more, with great effect –
Father Josef started writing (of his journeys, he'd reflect).

On Christmas Eve, his second year, the countryside was calling,
So Josef journeyed to the hills with favourite vistas sprawling;
"I'll bring my books and climb above the village for a viewing,"
A peaceful panorama was what Josef was pursuing.

Upon a knoll he stopped to rest, then set his rucksack down,
And seated on the earth to view the beauty all around;
The setting sun surrendered to the darkness of the eve,
And Josef marveled at the glory he would soon receive.

"The sky, she's never danced this way, with glitter, shining bright!
The gentle snow is colouring the town a radiant white!
The silence calms my spirit, gives my soul a peace, so mild
And there! The Christmas manger holds our Saviour, Heaven's child!"

As Josef looked in wonder at the holy scene below,
A narrow beam of light shone through the softly falling snow;
It glowed upon the Babe and drew the Father's gazes there
And left him genuflecting with the whispered words of prayer.

He took a quill and paper from his bag, without delay,
And wrote his thoughts in poetry, that eve of Christmas Day;
"The little babe, beside the church, His smile's a holy sight,"
Thought Josef as he wrote his poem that fateful, quiet night.

Two years ahead, in Oberndorf, his sermons he'd deliver,
As Josef served St. Nicholas Church, along the Salzach River;
And there, with chance, the preacher would befriend a choirmaster
Who shared his love of music during visits with the pastor.

That Christmas Eve, while choosing hymns to mark the celebration
Josef yearned for something new to give his congregation;
He called upon his choirmaster friend, with great desire,
"Franz Gruber, can you help create some music for our choir?"

So Josef shared his poem with Franz (it was their destiny),
Who, on that holy eve, composed a pretty melody.
They called on Franz's wife, and then, enclosed in candlelight,
Unveiled the first performance of their lovely "Silent Night'.

"O Franz," exclaimed his wife, "this hymn has touched me with its splendour!
"The music flows so peacefully; the lyrics, truly tender!
"While we will pass – the two of us will someday leave this earth –
"This song will live in celebrations of our Saviour's birth!"

In the quiet hills of Oberndorf, that wondrous Christmas Eve,
As Josef gathered with his flock – the Christ Child they'd receive –
Along with Franz, they gave a gift the world would adore
But couldn't know how much they'd touch the world evermore.

Josef Mohr began his life in poverty, it's true,
And that was how it ended, but before his life was through,
He gave the world a song of hope and love to last all lives,
And every year, on Christmas Eve, his "Silent Night" survives!

ABIGAIL'S CHRISTMAS

At the young age of twelve, Abigail was the oldest child in Sunshine Dwelling. An orphanage which housed nine other children, all of whom were six years of age or younger, it was home for all of them. Abigail lost her parents in a tragic mudslide when she was three, and she only partially remembered them. Four of the other eight children were abandoned at birth, three were the only survivors of a fire that destroyed their multi-family hut, and the others could no longer be cared for by ailing parents or relatives. With no family left for any of them, few visitors ever walked through the doors of the orphanage, and it left the younger ones, especially, lonesome. Abigail took it upon herself to be a friend to all of them.

For a young girl, her days were full, and busy. Abigail rose at 6:30 to begin every day with a few moments in silence, praying, "Dear Mother Mary, give me the strength, as you had, to accept God's plan for me, and to do it well. Help me to be a light in the lives of the other little children at Sunshine Dwelling, so that, somehow, I can lead them to a life that will be pleasing to God, and a life that will bring them great rewards in Heaven. I put all my faith in you, oh Blessed Mary, and I know that you will guide me, lead me, and watch over me. Amen."

While two adults were on hand to make meals, watch over all the children, and ensure that necessary supplies were available, Abigail always followed her morning prayers by helping each of the other children to get dressed, to make their beds, and to pray their morning rosary. She helped throughout the day with the meals for the little ones, ensuring that each was washed and clean afterwards. She played with them. She read to them. She comforted them if they were sad, or crying, holding them in her arms and rocking with them on an old wooden chair in the corner of their dormitory room, until they found rest, or sleep.

While Abigail was able to spend an hour each day after lunch at the village school, some of her favourite times were when she took the children on afternoon walks beyond the orphanage to a little creek at the edge of the village. Once there, the children would splash and play in the shallow stream, or sit on the grass along the gently flowing water, under glorious skies and in the midst of warm breezes. She always brought a bag of crackers, enough for one each, and they all shared in a drink of water from a single bottle that she always filled and brought from the orphanage. Sometimes, Abigail would carry a bag of extra clothing for them, if there was a breeze, and she would tell them stories of hope, assuring the children that their angels and God were always watching over them, so that the little ones would not succumb to occasional feelings of abandonment, or distress. She treasured their walks and their trips to the creek, because for those moments, at least – she hoped – the little children could enjoy their lives, and find peace and comfort in their otherwise monotonous days.

In the evenings, after reading them a bedtime story, Abigail would always sing one of her favourite hymns, *Whatsoever You Do*, to the children. She loved the song's lyrics, how it suggested that offering forms of kindness to ordinary people in her life was the same as offering that same kindness to Jesus. Abigail can still vaguely remember her mother singing this hymn to her as a young child, and she always feels her mother watching over her when she sings its lyrics. So softly, with the lights down low, and the children tucked into their bunks, Abigail would sing the words of the verses with beautiful rhythm, repeating the chorus after each one. By the time she reached the end of the song, if anyone still stirred or eyes were caught open, she hummed its lyrics until the last little boy or girl was sound asleep.

Then, as she did every evening, Abigail left the orphanage and walked thirty minutes from the little village to the country church. When she arrived, lights were still on and several candles were lit, and Sister Miriam always greeted her and welcomed her. "Blessings, dear child," she would say, adding, "Welcome! Welcome! We have been waiting for you. Come, kneel and pray."

Abigail loved Sister Miriam deeply, as her own mother. She saw her during masses and at Sunday School, where Sister

Miriam led the class discussions in her beautiful blue habit, and she so looked forward to Sister Miriam's visits to the village. One of her favourite lessons was Sister Miriam's early Advent teaching of how the heavens open on the eve of Christmas, and the angels descend along Jacob's Ladder, appearing to the precious few who have lived unblemished, honourable, and caring lives. Abigail secretly aspired to be recognized in such a way. But even more so, she longed for the peace she always felt in Sister Miriam's presence, and she once revealed to the gracious nun, "Your care for me and for others is a true gift, and it's helped me to feel God's call for me; one day I will be a servant of God, as you are!"

Abigail's visits to the church were not long, but she would always kneel at the front of the church, near the altar, where a wooden statue of a lovely angel stood. There, every evening, she knelt in prayer, thanking God for the day and for His blessings, asking Him to continue to watch over her and to help her in her life. "Please bring me content and peace," she would say, adding, "My days are long, but I love the little children so much. Watch over them, and help me to be for them whatever they need me to be. I want them to be happy, and safe, for I know that it is in their happiness that I, too, am happy." Abigail would finish with the *Angel of God* prayer, arise, and give Sister Miriam a warm hug before returning back to the village.

To be sure, life wasn't easy for the young girl; others her age surely led more carefree lives filled with play and adventure with family and friends. But Abigail's selfless nature, her deep care for others, her faith, compassion, and empathy all ensured that her life was a full one, and that, every day, she gave of her heart, of herself.

Now, the Advent season was quickly drawing to a close,

and at the dawn of this Christmas Eve, Abigail set out on her day as usual. Following her morning prayers, and after breakfast, she helped the others to wash up, and then she took them on a late morning walk to the creek. It was her Christmas present for them, for she knew how much they loved the sound and feel of the creek and its lovely surrounding meadows. Today, instead of crackers, Abigail presented each child with a simple sugar cookie that she helped prepare the night before when she had returned from church. Then she gave them each a picture which she had drawn in the weeks leading up to Christmas. Each was the same – a picture of the children playing beside the creek. That way, she thought, if weather, illness, or any other reason prevented one or all of them from walking to the creek one day, at least they could look at the pictures and see themselves there.

The children were so happy with the cookies and the beautiful pictures! They stayed near the creek into the afternoon of Christmas Eve, celebrating their togetherness and playing games and telling stories. Each child gave Abigail a heartfelt Christmas hug, and then together they sang *O Come All Ye Faithful* as they skipped, hand in hand, all the way back to Sunshine Dwelling.

Upon arrival, they enjoyed an early supper of ham, sweet potatoes, and vegetables and fruits of all kinds. Their two caretakers worked tirelessly since morning preparing the meal for them, gathering carrots, peas, corn, oranges, bananas, and pineapples from their garden. It was a real Christmas feast for the children, and they savoured it immensely.

Afterwards, they all cleaned off the table, washed and put away the dishes and gathered in the front room for the final time this year to light all four candles of their simple, but treasured Advent wreath. Sister Miriam had given the candles to the orphanage several years earlier, and they were only lit for one hour each day during the Advent season. Thin willow branches had once been collected and woven together to encircle little metal cups that held the candles. Four different children took turns each day lighting the candles, and today was Abigail's turn, along with the three youngest. A soft glow soon filled the room, and the children held hands and gently swayed in a circle, singing *O Come Divine Messiah, O Come O Come Emmanuel,* and *The Whole World is Waiting for Love,* among several others. Abigail had sung the songs with them in their room each day of Advent, and the children were now singing together like a polished children's choir! Pure delight filled the room, as Christmas Eve once again brought anticipation and hope to the children.

After the last song was finished, the children gathered close to Abigail as she knelt with them beside the Advent wreath, still holding hands. She then began a prayer, saying, "Lord, on this eve of your coming, we pray that you watch over us. We await your arrival with hope, and joy, and we look forward to celebrating your birth on Christmas morning!"

Abigail then softly blew out the four Advent candles, and as she tucked the younger ones into their beds, she told them, "Tomorrow we celebrate the birth of Jesus! Sleep well, for we will have much to celebrate in the morning!" At the end of a full day of song, activity, and a wonderful feast, Abigail only got through a few verses of her favourite night-time song before the children were all fast asleep.

The next morning, the children would gather again beside the wreath to sing *Happy Birthday* to the Baby Jesus, before enjoying a Christmas Day visit from Sister Miriam. For now, however, Abigail was preparing to leave to celebrate Christmas Eve service at the country church. She put on her best clothes – a long rose-coloured skirt and a long-sleeved white blouse, a gift she received the previous year from Sister Miriam, who had her own sister create it just for Abigail. On her feet she wore her black sandals, which she scrubbed and polished earlier that morning. It was a beautiful outfit, and she wore it proudly, smiling as she looked at herself in her mirror, before brushing her hair and hurrying out on her thirty minute journey.

The sun was setting as she approached the church, and Sister Miriam was in the entrance to welcome her as she arrived. "Merry Christmas, dear one," Sister Miriam said with a hug, and then together they walked to the front pew, where they knelt in prayer for a few moments before the service began. The church was full, and Abigail listened intently to the readings, and joined in enthusiastically and devotedly with the singing of the hymns. She absorbed the words of Luke's Gospel, and imagined, in detail, being there on that first Christmas morning, walking with the shepherds and cozying with the animals to welcome and witness the birth of Christ.

At the end of the service, before departing, Abigail approached the wooden angel and knelt in prayer. She began to whisper the *Angel of God* prayer, as she did every evening, but she used different words this time, ones she had written herself and rehearsed throughout the Advent season. Softly, Abigail prayed, "Angel of Christmas, my guardian dear, to whom Christ's birth commits me here, ever the year be at my side, to help keep the spirit of Christmastide. Amen." Abigail then added, "Welcome, Dear Lord! Please watch over the little children of all the world, but especially those at Sunshine Dwelling. Help me to do your work, and to bring them peace by leading them to you. And one more thing – Happy Birthday, Jesus!"

Abigail rose, then, with a smile and a look of complete peace, and walked back towards the entrance of the church. With a wish for a peaceful and wonderful Christmas, she hugged Sister Miriam, who said, "Blessings be yours, dear Abigail. The Lord is pleased with what you do, and how you watch over the little children. May this be your most wonderful Christmas, yet!" With that, Abigail descended the steps from the church entrance and began her thirty minute walk back to the orphanage.

By now, the earth was dark, but skies were clear, and moonlight penetrated the darkness and cast a dim glow over the countryside. Countless stars twinkled overhead and seemed to follow her as she walked through near darkness over the gently rolling hills and meadows back to the village.

Abigail had come about halfway back along the trail from the church when she suddenly stopped, startled. In front of her, high over the hills that surrounded her on the trail back to the village, the heavens had parted, and a host of angels was descending on a glorious winding golden staircase. They glowed white and gold and yellow. Some played flutes while others held harps or little guitars, and they all seemed to flow gently down the staircase, and their smiles and outstretched arms brought Abigail a feeling of overwhelming calmness and peace. The young girl fell to her knees and brought her hands together in prayer, when the angel who first reached the bottom of the staircase gently put his hand on her shoulder and said, "Dear child, we come as God's gift to you this Christmas Eve. Rejoice! The Lord your Saviour has arrived on this most holy night. And indeed, He is so pleased with you. All the things you do for the children of Sunshine Dwelling you also do for Jesus! Your faith, your devotion, and most importantly, your love for the children bring Him such delight! Your life is simple but it is full, and because you give so much of yourself, you receive blessings in return. So willingly, you show the spirit of Christmas by giving from your heart not only at Christmas, but *every* day. Truly, you are a child of God, and you are answering His call, just as Mary did. Your life is pure, and on this Holy Christmas Eve, I promise you, we are with you always, and we will be with you until the day God brings you home. So go, and enjoy the peace and hope that is Christmas. And continue to love others as God loves you."

With that, the staircase receded to the heavens, as did the angels, and Abigail heard them softly singing *Joy to the World* as they looked down upon her and disappeared into the sky. When the heavens closed, she fell prone upon the ground, on the cool grass.

Gathering herself, Abigail slowly rose and gazed into the Christmas Eve sky. "The angels have come to me on Jacob's Ladder," she whispered to herself, remembering her Sunday School discussions with Sister Miriam earlier in Advent, adding, "On this Christmas Eve, truly the Lord Jesus is *here!*" Knowing that the angels, and indeed, God, were always watching over her, and that they were genuinely pleased with her help in the orphanage, and with her faith and her desire to answer the call to live a life devoted to God, Abigail began a slow and gentle skip the rest of the way back. Her heart was light, her path was clear. And on this calm, most holy night, she received a rare gift that will carry her with great hope through the rest of her childhood and towards a life of deep fulfillment and inner peace.

In bed that night, Abigail thought, "Sister Miriam was right – this *has* been my most wonderful Christmas ever! Oh, I can't wait to tell her all about it in the morning!" She rolled over and smiled in the light of a bright star that shone through the window. With peaceful content, Abigail drifted into sleep and dreamed of her little friends at Sunshine Dwelling, and of sharing with them the gift that she had received on this special Christmas Eve, and the wonders of Christmas Day to come.

LOWLY SHEPHERD

Lowly shepherd, with his sheep, on rolling countryside;
With wooden staff, he cares for them - most humble, worthy guide.
A strip of leather wraps his feet to keep his sandals set;
A weathered robe flows round him in a moonlight silhouette.

Uneducated, simple, there's a beard upon his face;
Humility has given him a heart that's filled with grace.
He wants for nothing – pleased to guard his flock through day and night,
Not knowing he's been chosen to receive a gift tonight.

He gathers near another, as their flock is resting, still;
They watch in silence in the night - on guard upon the hill.
A little fire, glowing, brings some comfort in the night;
When overhead, the darkened sky is pierced with holy light….

Their faces tell of terror as they stumble to their knees;
The blazing light of glory has them wishing they could flee.
But in their fear, an angel comes with news of greatest joy –
"Fear not, for near, in Bethlehem, is born a little boy!

"A saviour for the world – greatest gift from God on high –
Is given you in silence on this oh, most holy nigh'!"
A multitude of angels then proclaims the blessed birth,
With glories sung to God and hopes for peace upon the earth.

In faith, they go together, with the news of birth, His gift –
In search of such a wonder, to the holy star they drift.
The little town of Bethlehem is where they find the Child,
Asleep atop a manger, with a pure, angelic smile.

A mule and a donkey fill the corners of the cave;
A cow is breathing warmly on the One who came to save.
His mother and his father kneel upon the strawy floor;
Between them, so serenely, lies the One that they adore.

The simple shepherd enters, humbly kneeling 'fore the Lord,
"I give to you my heart – the only gift I can afford."
A smile from the Babe, with favour for the gift received,
Gives jubilation to the man who heard and then believed.

Rising, then, he leaves to share the gift he's found this night;
An overwhelming joy is spread through morning's coming light.
The promise of salvation has appeared upon the earth,
Arriving Christmas morning with the Holy Child's birth.

Lowly shepherd, chosen for a gift of consequence;
The angel's proclamation, he embraced in confidence.
Believing, he was first to see God's gift on Christmas morn' –
Salvation in a stable where the Baby Christ was born.

CHRISTMAS FOR CLEMENT

Is there a more joyful time of the year in the eyes of an eight year old boy than the remaining days of Advent leading up to the blessed glories of Christmas? Certainly, to Clement, with all that was going on in his little country school to prepare for Christmas, it really was a time of wonder, imagination, and eager anticipation.

Clement was the oldest of three children. He had one younger brother, Solomon, who was in Grade 1, and a sister, Magdala-Marie, who would have to wait one more year to begin school with her brothers. They lived in a small but charming farmhouse in the gently rolling hills just outside the little country village of Wonder Brook. There, along with their dogs Cocoa and Trixie, two-year-old Golden Retrievers, and their family cat Patches, there was never a dull moment. Countless were the spring and summer days that Clement would take his younger siblings playing, rambling, and chasing one another through the hilly fields beside their farm, or climbing the big oak tree that stood proudly in the midst of the yard behind their house, to reach the little fort that their father had built in its branches, or to see beyond the fields to Pleasant Pond and the little creek that meandered away from it. Sometimes, their parents would come along and the children would splash in the shallow waters of the stream, or wade into the cooling waters of the pond. What a way for a child to spend a summer evening in the countryside!

In the autumn, when the red and golden leaves had fallen from the majestic sprawling tree, Clement raked them together in huge piles and then the three of them took turns jumping from the tire swing to splash into huge splatterings of leaves. The joy and laughter of those crisp autumn afternoons were treasured, cherished moments that brought all-embracing happiness to each of the children.

And then, when the first snows arrived and began to paint the countryside in a spotless white that sparkled and gleamed in the nighttime moonlight, the children would layer themselves with shirts and sweaters, don their knitted coats, toques, scarves, and mitts, pull on their toasty warm winter boots and, together with their beloved animal friends, Clement would lead them stomping through the fields and making paths to their favourite spots, like the huge boulder beside the fence in the corner of the yard, or – of course – to the large oak tree. Truly, childhood on the farm in the valley of Wonder Brook, for Clement, Solomon, and Magdala-Marie, was a special, magical time, indeed!

Clement was approaching his third Christmas break at

Wonder Brook School. His class of fourteen students was the largest in the school, and during this last week of classes before winter holidays, the spirit of Christmas had embraced every room, every hall, and indeed, every person – teacher and student, alike – within the walls of the school. Christmas music and melodies played out from every room – oh, how Clement loved the songs and hymns of Christmas! Truly, Clement loved music, and singing, in general. But as soon as the autumn snows carpeted the valleys and hills around Wonder Brook, he began sifting through his parents' collection of Christmas records and let the wonderful music and his passionate singing echo throughout his family's farmhouse. So while all of the elementary grades could be frequently heard singing simple carols like *Hark the Herald Angels Sing* and *Away in a Manger* during those final days before Christmas, it was Clement's voice that was always filled with the most spirit, spreading in tune throughout the room and down the hall!

Along with the music and singing, great wreaths of evergreen and holly filled the hallway walls, connected by flowing garland hung neatly in between, and a life-size nativity scene was set up inside the main entrance, so that every student, teacher, and visitor alike could enjoy it and witness the true meaning of Christmas whenever they entered the building. There really was no mistaking what season it was, and everyone, particularly Clement, wholeheartedly welcomed it!

As the second last day before Christmas break drew to a close, Clement's teacher, Miss Hopkins, gave her students a special assignment to end their Advent celebrations and prepare them for the start of the holiday season. "Children, the great and holy Christmas season is almost upon us. We have done well with our prayers and our songs and celebrations during Advent to get us ready for the birth of Jesus. Before we end our Advent preparations, I would like each of you to come to school tomorrow with a response to the following statement – 'What Christmas Means To Me'. It doesn't have to be long, but if you could prepare a couple of sentences for your response, we will end our final day of classes by sharing your thoughts with everyone. Take some time to really think about your replies, and look inside your hearts and souls to find an answer that will best describe what you hear from within."

With that, Miss Hopkins blew out the candles of the Advent Wreath that had sat on her desk since the beginning of the season. The children filed out into the hall to gather their winter coats and boots and were passing the nativity scene and spreading out beyond the front doors of the school. Clement held Solomon's hand as they set out on their half-mile walk home. "One more day! One more day," exclaimed Solomon, eager for the start of the Christmas season. Clement smiled and hugged his little brother, saying, "You're right – Jesus will be here soon! Christmas is such a wonderful time of the year!"

Together, the two boys skipped along the side of the road to the edge of town and then along the country road to their little farmhouse. Cocoa, Trixie, and Patches all came to greet them with wagging tails and wet kisses. Magdala-Marie stood in the front porch, welcoming them with a bright smile and a warm hug, and their mother stood near her in the kitchen, saying, "Welcome home, my little angels!"

The whole house smelled of gingerbread, shortcake, and pumpkin spice, and a warm fire glowed, popped, and danced in the living room, not far from their glorious tree, which was layered with tinsel and covered with treasured home-made ornaments and topped with their keepsake angel. The Christmas tree filled the room with the sweet smell of fir, and beside it, their old record player was softly playing Christmas favourites that were echoing now throughout the house, and really bringing the joy of Christmas into Clement's heart.

Before Clement took off his boots, he said to his mother, "Miss Hopkins gave us a little assignment for tomorrow. We've each been asked to tell the class what our response would be to 'What Christmas Means to Me'. It sounded simple at first, but as I thought about it, I realized that Christmas means *many* things to me. It means love, and family, and happiness, and giving, and celebration. Oh, I could go on and on. How can I give a reply of only one or two sentences?"

"I have an idea," his mother said. "Why don't you walk to the church. The Christmas choir is practicing right now, but you can sit in solitude and let God bring your answer to you."

"Of course," Clement replied. It was always in the church that he found peace, and clarity, and where he was able to openly pray from his heart in silence. "Thank you, Mother. I will go right away. I won't be long. But I know that I'll find what I'm looking for!"

Clement quickly stepped out from the porch, closed the door behind him, and walked down the short flight of stairs from the front of their home. Though flurries were gently falling about, the trees were still, and the mild winter late afternoon made it an easy walk to the church, even in the disappearing daylight.

Soon Clement had reached the edge of town, and the lovely brick church that stood there. A beautiful glow shone through the colourful stained glass windows that sat amidst the brown bricks of the side walls of the church, and up the walls of the square steeple. A soft covering of snow clung to the steep slopes of the rooftop, and the Holy Family sat in the covering of a wooden stable that was placed between the church and the woods of the nearby forest.

As Clement approached the church, the sound of carols grew louder, and he could hear the choir from within, and the accompaniment of the organ and the bells. It was a lovely sound, and as he entered the doors to the church, it grew and danced throughout the vaulted, arched ceiling of the sanctuary, and echoed clearly all around. He stood there for a moment in the church entryway, closing his eyes and letting a big smile form on his face as the music of Christmas filled his soul.

Clement then stood at the entrance to the sanctuary. A rich red carpet spread out before him all the way to the altar between two aisles of pews, each ten rows long and wide enough to hold about five or six parishioners, just enough to be cozy when the church was full. The ends of the pews along the centre aisle were decorated with garland and bright red holly berries and a single thick white candle that stood atop a golden rod and glowed softly at the edge of the pew. Halfway down along each side of the sanctuary, a square pillar of brick stood as a support, reaching from the floor to the arched ceiling above. Each was decorated with simple sprigs of evergreen, and each embraced a golden stand in its corner with the side wall that held five white candles, whose flames danced and cast shadows across the bricks.

The centre aisle drew the eye towards the altar, which was small, but still wonderfully decorated. A red cloth covered the altar, and two smaller stands – each holding five smaller white candles, and decorated with holly and garland, stood on each side of the altar. Five flourishing poinsettias sat in pots that were decorated green, in front of the altar, and the chestnut brown wooden pulpit stood to the right side, its ten steps leading readers high above the pews. Behind the altar stood the magnificent scene of Bethlehem, as three large, stained glass panels depicted the Holy Family in the middle and the shepherds and wise men on either side, with the Star of Bethlehem overhead. The ceiling of the church was filled with dark brown arched beams, rising from the walls of brick on either side. The entire scene was magnificent, and Clement gazed upon it in wonder.

At the entrance to the sanctuary where Clement now stood, the choir loft filled the space over the entryway to the church, and extended beyond the first two rows of pews. The front of its railing extended into the sanctuary and was covered with flowing garland and evergreen, and the choir members stood there in their white gowns, holding their red songbooks in front of them, rehearsing for Christmas Eve.

Clement walked up along the right side and sat in the fifth row of pews along the side wall, near the stand of five candles. He genuflected towards the altar, and knelt in front of the pew. With an innocent and honest heart, he whispered, "Dear God. We are again about to celebrate the wonderful gift that you gave us all – your only son. Truly, this is the reason we rejoice at Christmas, and there are so many wonderful experiences that bring meaning to this blessed season. Please help me to find in my heart a special answer to the assignment that Miss Hopkins gave us today – 'What Christmas Means to Me'."

With that, Clement sat back in the pew. Halos surrounded the yellow flicker of the candles throughout the church and cast the only light, but it danced warmly on the brown of the brick and wood of the building, and brought a cozy feeling of content to Clement. He glanced through the colourful stained glass and could see snowflakes still gently falling outside. The choir began its rehearsal of "Oh Holy

Night", and Clement felt complete comfort, and silently slipped into a later-afternoon daydream.

Clement saw himself encircled by a host of twelve angels. They floated gently about him as he sat in the pew, their flowing white robes reaching beyond their feet, and their little wings slowly fluttering as they hovered easily over him. Very softly he could hear them murmur the singing of "Oh Come, Little Children". How beautiful it sounded, as the choir of angels tenderly sang a hymn of Christmas to Clement! He sensed warmth growing in his chest. No, it was in his heart! Yes, Clement felt a warming sensation in his heart with the sound of the angels singing. "What a wonderful feeling of kindliness," Clement thought in his dream, as he stared at the angels while they slowly circled round him, singing their hymn with affection.

As the angels ended their song, Clement then felt another sensation, again in his heart. He turned his gaze from the angels around him towards his chest, as he gently held it in his left hand. Feeling the rhythmic beating of his heart, Clement somehow heard the angels as they spoke to him.

"Young boy," they said, "Truly, the spirit of Christmas is within your heart. The love and care that you show for your family and for God's creatures captures the essence of Christmas. You find beauty in the music of the carols of Christmas, and their wonderful lyrics. You give of your heart, and that is all that God asks of you. The infant Jesus will be here again soon, the greatest gift for all people of the world. Rejoice in it, and share the joy in your heart with everyone you see, for then you will be spreading the spirit of Christmas, as you give of your heart, and from your soul. Merry Christmas, Clement!"

Clement's eyes flickered a few times, and then opened. As his vision cleared, he saw that the angels he had dreamed of were gone. But truly, he knew, they *were* there for a moment, singing to him, and speaking to him in his heart.

Clement got up and exited the pew, genuflected once more, and then walked along the side aisle back to the entryway of the church. His heart felt so light because of the angels that came to him in his dream. He knew exactly what he would tell the class tomorrow, and as the door to the church closed behind him, he ran along the country road all the way home.

As he entered the porch, his father greeted him, "Welcome home, dear son. I understand you've been at church, and praying. I trust that you found what you were looking for!"

"Indeed, Father," Clement replied. "As always, I found an answer to my prayers in our church, and what a wonderful answer it was!" Clement explained his entire experience to everyone as they gathered for supper. "Oh Clement," his mother said, "I'm so happy for you. Indeed, the angels of heaven are watching over you!"

Solomon and Magdala-Marie rose to hug Clement, saying, "What a wonderful gift to receive at Christmas! Miss Hopkins will be so happy to hear your answer tomorrow!"

The following day came soon enough, and as Clement and Solomon enjoyed their last day of classes before the Christmas break, Clement watched as the clock above the door of his classroom finally showed 2:30. The time had come for the children to share their responses to Miss Hopkins' question about the meaning of Christmas.

Clement sat patiently as he heard classmates share their

answers to the class. Family get-togethers, playing with friends, sledding on the hills, Christmas feasts, gatherings at church, staying up late, giving and receiving gifts, and cozying by fireplaces while listening to the story of Christmas, were answers given by the children of his class, with some of the responses being repeated by many of them.

At last, Clement was called upon to give his answer.

"Well, Clement, that leaves you," Miss Hopkins prompted him. "Can you please share with us what Christmas means to you?"

Clement walked up to the front of the room and then turned to his classmates, and to Miss Hopkins, who stood at the back of the room, near her desk.

With his fingers interlocked as if in prayer, Clement timidly looked across the room at the faces of the other students, and then to Miss Hopkins, and then began to give his response, saying, "Christmas to me means everything that you've all said, and so much more. God gave me – and all of us – a friend that will walk with us every day of our lives. That's pretty important, and that's the most important gift of Christmas. But beyond all this, to me, Christmas means even more. To me, Christmas is a sound – it's the wonderful sound of hearing angels sing! And still, there's a little bit more. If I listen real carefully, Christmas, to me, is hearing angels speaking in my heart."

On the way back to his desk, Clement looked up at Miss Hopkins and he watched as a tear trickled towards the smile on her face. She looked at him with a loving gaze, feeling a lump in her throat, and as Clement walked past her, she whispered to him, "That was so lovely, Clement. Thank you."

The clock now showed 3:00, and there was just enough time for the entire class to sing *Silent Night* and then *Joy to the World*, before the final bell. Miss Hopkins said to the class before they left, "Thank you, children. You did a marvelous job of sharing your thoughts on what Christmas means to you. I will remember your answers always, and indeed, they have been a wonderful present for me this Christmas. Have a very Merry Christmas, everyone!"

The children together said, "Merry Christmas to you, too, Miss Hopkins," and then they gathered their things and headed out the front doors of the school.

Clement again held Solomon's hand as the two of them skipped all the way home. Cocoa, Trixie, and Patches greeted them as always, with tails wagging and tongues kissing, and Magdala-Marie hugged them both as they entered the porch. "Merry Christmas Clement! Merry Christmas, Solomon," she said, as her mother smiled behind her.

"Welcome home, my boys," she said, helping them take off their coats and mitts. "And Merry Christmas!"

Having received his gifts from the angels the afternoon before, and then sharing his response to the class just moments ago, Clement felt the spirit of Christmas well up inside even more so than at any time during the past several weeks. Remembering their sound of singing, and the sound of them speaking in his heart, Clement hurried towards the music of the living room. The joyous hymns reminded him of the church choir that he listened to only yesterday, and the heavenly gift of angels that he had received. "What a wonderful present," he thought, as he turned around to his family, echoing their sentiment, exclaiming, "And Merry Christmas to all of you! Indeed! Merry Christmas!"

JOSEPH'S DREAM

It's Christmastime, and once again, the Greatest Story Told,
Brings peace, and hope – at Bethlehem is where it will unfold;
We read of how a manger scene embraced our Saviour's birth,
And how the Holy Family kindled joy throughout the earth.

But hidden in that story, for he almost goes unseen,
A gentle man, a righteous man is central to the scene;
No words he spoke in scripture, but 'twas God who spoke *to him*,
And guided Joseph to that fateful eve in Bethlehem.

Vowed to Mary, marriage is the calling that they share,
Till quietly, in Nazareth, an angel would declare,
"You'll bear an infant of the Holy Spirit, from on high!"
"Then let it be…," was Mary's most obedient reply.

Joseph learns from Mary – his betrothed, the Virgin, mild –
The overwhelming news that, of the Spirit, she's with child.
He's given an impasse, for whose solution, how he prayed –
Not knowing what would follow from the choice that Joseph made.

Continue with the marriage or discreetly separate?
Save Mary from disgrace or lawfully repudiate?
He knows he *must* protect her from assured humiliation,
Or penalty of stoning, such a cruel demonstration.

Thinking on this quandary and how to best proceed,
Joseph waits and trusts the Lord will somehow intercede;
And then, in dream, from God the angel Gabriel appears,
And gives a needed resolution, easing Joseph's fears:

"Be not afraid, for by the Holy Spirit she's conceived –
"A gift from Heaven, Mary has so graciously received;
"So take her as your wife and help to raise the boy within,
"And call him 'Jesus', for he'll save his people from their sins."

Joseph woke from dream and followed Gabriel's command,
To Bethlehem he went with Mary, as the Lord had planned.
The Babe was born to Mary, highly honoured mother, mild,
And Joseph, willingly, the earthly father of the child.

A miracle resulted from the choice that Joseph made;
Oh, what we would have missed if he instead had been afraid!
His choice fulfilled Isaiah's words, that very first Noel,
And gave the world a saviour with the name, Emmanuel.

CHRISTMAS AND THE SHEPHERD BOY

Madelyn slipped on her black dress shoes, tying the black buckles behind her ankles. With her white stockings and her red dress, and the pretty little white and green bow in her dark hair, she looked Christmassy and classy as she sat patiently waiting to go to the Christmas Eve service. Along with her parents, for the first time since she was a baby, she was visiting her grandparents for the holidays, and she was excited about going to Mass on her grandparents' sleigh to the old country church, and to listening to her grandfather sing in the Christmas Eve choir.

It was a short trip to the church, less than 20 minutes, and it was just below zero – the warm coats, mitts, and ear muffs made the journey comfortable for all of the riders, and the heavy wool blankets that were shared by the members of each row of the sleigh made it very cozy indeed. The horses knew the way, so Madelyn's grandfather asked her parents to take the reins in the front row, letting the horses follow the tracks through the rolling countryside to the church, so that Madelyn could enjoy the ride in the second row with her grandparents.

They were going early, so that Madelyn's grandfather could join the choir in some last-minute rehearsals before taking their places and beginning the opening carols prior to the start of the Mass. As the horses turned away from the lane and into the country, Madelyn thought of the carols that the choir would be singing, and she said to her grandparents, "I'm so happy to be joining you for Christmas. It is my favourite time of year, for so many reasons; but I think most of all, I love Christmas because of the music and the carols. They are all so wonderful, especially the ones that talk of peace, joy, love, and remembering that holy night in Bethlehem when Jesus was born!"

"Oh, Madelyn," her grandmother answered, "Your love for Christmas is very admirable. You are wise beyond your 8 years for seeing and understanding the true reason for celebrating Christmas!"

Her grandfather then added, "Yes, Madelyn, your grandmother and I are very happy that you are spending Christmas with us, and that you and your parents can join us at the Christmas Eve service. It is my favourite Mass, and I just love being able to share my voice and to help to lead the singing of the wonderful carols of Christmas!"

Madelyn replied, "I'm so excited, Grandpa, to hear you sing, and to sing along too, with you, Grandma, Mom and Dad, and the choir."

And then, Madelyn thought of something. Looking up to her grandfather, she said, "Say, Grandpa, there are so many beautiful carols that are sung at a Christmas Eve service, from

Silent Night and *O Holy Night* to *O Come all ye Faithful* and *Joy to the World*, and even others, that are all really lovely. But, I was wondering, is there a song that might mean just a little bit more to you? Perhaps one that is just a little bit more of a favourite for you?"

Madelyn's grandmother smiled, for she knew the answer, and she winked at Madelyn, as her husband began his answer.

"Yes, Madelyn," her grandfather started, "it's true – I love to sing *all* of the carols at Christmas. But there *is* one that means just a little bit more to me. It's called *Transeamus Usque Bethlehem*. It's a Latin song whose title means 'Let us go to Bethlehem'. Not many churches sing it, but I've known that carol for more than 60 years – most of my life; it tells of the Christmas Eve shepherds and how they responded to the Word of the angel and hurried to Bethlehem to see the Holy Family. It was *my* grandfather's favourite Christmas song. He used to sing it in *his* church's Christmas Eve choir, and it is one that our choir will sing tonight. We have been singing it on Christmas Eve for as long as I've been in the choir, over 40 years!"

"Wow, Grandpa," Madelyn began her reply, adding, "That is quite a tradition that started with your own grandfather and that you've been carrying on all these years! I can see why this song means so much to you! Maybe *I* will get to sing it in a choir when I get older."

"That would be wonderful," Madelyn's grandmother replied, adding, "You have a beautiful voice, and you will be a welcome addition to any choir! Your grandfather really does love that song, and he has for a long, long time." Then, looking at her husband, and winking now to *him*, she said, "And I think he might share with you another reason why it means so much to him."

"What is it, Grandpa," Madelyn inquired, adding, "Why else is this song so special to you?"

"Madelyn," her grandfather replied, "As I told you, my grandfather used to sing that song in his church's choir, and he is the one who introduced it to me. But my grandfather once told me a story about the song, a very special story. And yes, it is time now that you hear it."

Madelyn's grandparents smiled at each other and at their granddaughter, and hearing their conversation, Madelyn's parents looked back towards her and also smiled at their daughter, and then they all sat attentively to listen to Madelyn's grandfather's story.

"My grandfather sat me down one Christmas Eve morning," he began, "when I was 8 or 9, just as old as you, Madelyn. He said he had a story to tell me about the priest at his church, Father Eli. The priest was an elderly man, but he still played the guitar and the organ, and he helped to direct their choir.

"Well, Father Eli spent one Christmas in the Holy Land, in the city of Jerusalem. In the afternoon of Christmas Eve, he was walking on a path a few kilometres south of the city, among olive groves, shrubs and low rolling hills of sparse vegetation. Father Eli was on his way to Bethlehem for the Christmas Eve service, and on his way, he saw a young shepherd boy approach with his walking pole. When they met, the young boy noticed the man's collar and said to him, 'Hello Father, and Merry Christmas. If you have a few moments, there is a story I would like to tell you. Today is the anniversary of something very special that happened near here last year, on Christmas Eve.'

"Father Eli was intrigued, and he said to the boy, 'What is

it? What has happened that you speak of?'

"The boy answered Father Eli, telling him his story."

'I was in these hills last Christmas Eve, with my father, his two brothers, and three of their cousins, all of them shepherds. The sheep were in the fields, and I was helping to watch over them. Behind that olive tree on the hillside before us, a peaceful figure came out, glowing in the evening twilight, and it smiled at us. He moved towards us slowly and steadily, but none of us were afraid. Instead, the figure spoke to us with a gentle voice; he told us that his friends were coming, and that they wanted to celebrate the anniversary of Christ's birth. He said that shepherds in these very hills were approached by an angel on the first Christmas Eve, and upon hearing its words, they hurried to Bethlehem to see the Holy Family that would be resting there. He then said that he and his friends wanted to sing a song to celebrate that first Christmas Eve, and he began to speak the lyrics to my father, my uncles, and their cousins; the words were in Latin, but the men quickly learned them, and the figure told us the meaning of the words. All of them happily agreed that they would help the glowing figure; with its direction, they rehearsed the song several times, and then the figure started leading us down the hills toward Bethlehem. Just as we began walking behind it, dozens of other glowing figures – Heaven's angels – appeared and hovered overhead, following us. Some of them had harps, some had flutes, and some even had guitars. At one point, the figure leading us stopped, turned to face everyone, spread his arms wide overhead, and simply nodded. At once, the music began, and not long after, lovely voices filled these hills.

'The shepherds started out; their voices were clear and strong, floating towards the little town and spreading throughout the valley, as they first sang these words that the glowing figure taught them:

Transeamus usque Bethlehem, Et videamus hoc verbum quod factum est – Mariam et Joseph et Infantum positum in praesepio. The words of this verse mean, *Let us go to Bethlehem, and behold the Word that has been presented to us – Mary and Joseph, and the Child, placed in a manger*!

'And then, the most beautiful, clear, and lovely voices followed those of the shepherds, as the group of angels sang:

Gloria, Gloria in Excelsis Deo; Gloria, Gloria et in terra pax hominibus Bonae voluntatis, et in terra pax. These words mean, *Glory, Glory be to God on High; Glory, Glory and peace to all people of good will, and peace on Earth*!

'But Father, as overwhelming and moving as each group's verse was – both the shepherds and the angels – what followed was even more stirring, melodic, and harmonious. The shepherds and the angels sang the next verses *together*, with their voices intermingling to produce the most clear and lovely sound that I've ever heard.

'The angels sang their full *Gloria*, as before, while the shepherds sang:

Transeamus; audiamus multitudinem militiae coelestis laudantium Deum, which means, *Let us go; hear the crowd of Heavenly hosts who praise God*! To that, the shepherds added their line, *Mariam et Joseph et Infantum positum in praesepio*.

'Back and forth, and often together, *Transeamus* and *Gloria* were sung simultaneously with playfully falling and rising notes – especially of the angels' *Gloria* – that reached to the Heavens, while the other words of the lines were repeated and blended together. With the angels' final *Gloria*, the shepherds sang, *Transeamus et videamus quod factum est*, which means, *Let us go and see what has happened.*

'All the way into Bethlehem, the shepherds and the angels repeated this song, overlapping the shepherds' *Transeamus* lines with the angels' *Gloria* lines. It was such a lovely blending of harmonies, and perhaps the most melodious choir that has ever sung!

'Then, upon reaching Bethlehem, the angels dispersed and faded into the darkness. The shepherds and I continued towards an outdoors crèche on a corner near the Church of the Nativity, and we knelt down to pray to the Holy Family, just as the shepherds did that first Christmas Eve. And the glowing figure that led us all to Bethlehem from the Judean hills smiled towards us and then turned around and began walking back towards the countryside, before disappearing out of view.

'These hills are very special, Father. I don't know if the angels will ever return, but I hope one day, when I'm older and walking these trails, that they might appear and ask me to join them in singing of the shepherds on that first Christmas Eve!'"

Madelyn's grandfather then turned to her and said, "So you see, Madelyn, because of Father Eli's encounter with the shepherd boy, as told to your great-great-grandfather, *Transeamus Usque Bethlehem* has a very special meaning to me. Just as the shepherds on the first Christmas Eve heard the Word from an angel and hurried to Bethlehem to greet the Holy Family, the shepherds in Father Eli's story also went to Bethlehem on Christmas Eve, and together with a host of Heaven's angels, a melodious choir sang *Transeamus Usque Bethlehem* over and over through the Judean hills and all the way into Bethlehem! And so, every Christmas Eve when I sing this song with the choir, I imagine that I have the courage of the shepherds to take the Word from angels, go to Bethlehem, and rejoice at the birth of Jesus."

Madelyn smiled at her grandfather with tears on her cheek, as they arrived at the little country church and went inside. Her grandfather walked the stairs in the entrance up to the choir loft, while Madelyn, her grandmother, and her parents walked down the centre aisle, genuflecting beside a pew and then walking in to nearly fill the row. Madelyn looked around and admired the decorations. Two red candles sat in golden holders on the shelves inside each of the two windows on either side; bright red holly and green garland were hung on each of the pillars along the side walls; an intricate paper angel was clipped to each pew along the centre aisle; three evergreen trees stood in a triangle on one side of the altar; and beneath the trees, the Holy Family – along with shepherds, sheep, an oxen, a goat, and a mule – rested. Madelyn turned to her grandmother and whispered, "The church looks so beautiful, Grandma. I think Christmas has arrived!"

Madelyn's grandmother nodded and whispered back to her, "Yes, Madelyn, it sure does look lovely."

And then, an organ and a guitar started to play. Madelyn looked up and saw her grandfather behind her at the front of the loft, with seven other men standing side by side in front of a black railing above the back third of the congregation; all of them wore dashing black suits with dark red ties. Along both side walls, two narrow extensions of the loft reached another ten feet into the main body of the church. Five ladies stood shoulder to shoulder in both of the loft extensions – with each group facing the other across the church – and all of them wore white flowing cassocks.

With parishioners steadily arriving, the choir began their

introductory Christmas carols, inviting everyone to join in. They started with *The First Noel*, and then *Hark the Herald Angels Sing*. Then they sang *Mary's Boy Child, Angels We Have Heard on High, Away in a Manger, O Little Town of Bethlehem*, and *Somewhere in the Night*. Madelyn sang with all of her heart and soul, as the choir's strong and clear voices reverberated throughout the church and led everyone in song.

During the last two songs, the priest, the altar servers, and a deacon began to gather at the back of the church. There were still a few minutes before the procession would begin, but there was a short, noticeable pause after the last song that the choir sang. Something then happened that moved Madelyn, and, for the second time that evening, brought a few tiny tears of joy trickling down her cheeks.

The organ, joined now by a violin, started to play a very rhythmic and lovely melody, and the congregation became completely silent. The men in the choir, after the prelude, started singing the shepherds' verse of *Transeamus Usque Bethlehem*. Madelyn's eyes widened when she heard the men – and her grandfather – begin their verse. Her mother, on one side, reached to hold her left hand, while her grandmother, on the other side, held her right hand. Madelyn then closed her eyes and listened to – and embraced – the singing. The women in the choir soon began the angels' verse with the *Gloria*, and shortly afterwards, the 'shepherds' and the 'angels' were blending their lines together with a rhythmical and moving four-part harmony that resounded throughout the church. During the song, the congregation remained silent, and it was only the tenor and bass of the male choir voices from behind and the alto and soprano of the female choir voices from the sides that merged to fill the church with a clear, powerful, and sometimes playfully melodious anthem. Throughout all of it,

Madelyn clearly imagined the story of the shepherd boy and Father Eli, and she pictured herself sitting in the hills of Judea, listening to the heavenly choir above her.

As the song wound down, and the tears reached the bottom of Madelyn's cheeks, she squeezed both of the hands that were holding hers. She looked to her father, who smiled at her with a wink. She looked to her mother, who smiled and wiped the tears from both sides of Madelyn's face. She turned to the other side, smiled at her grandmother, and whispered, "I think this will be the best Christmas ever!" She then turned and looked up and over her shoulder at her grandfather, and, catching his eye, mouthed the words, "Thank you."

Madelyn went on to enjoy a peaceful and joyous Christmas gathering at her grandparents' country home, and one that she would never forget. Other Christmases came and went, and each had its own special moments and memories. But her 8th Christmas, the one spent at her grandparents' farm when she heard her grandfather's story of Father Eli and the shepherd boy – and the wonderful beauty of the song, *Transeamus Usque Bethlehem* – would be her favourite. She cherished it, and when the time came, she shared the story with her own children and grandchildren, ensuring that her grandfather's story, and the story of the shepherd boy, would live on.

Derek Becher

THE BELL TOWER CHERUBS

Nighttime rolls along the land and dims the fields dark,
It hushes sounds of wand'ring beasts, and warblings of the lark;
Serenity and silence ends the hustle that was there,
And now a starry stillness hangs in late December's air.

And soon, this night in Bethlehem, a scene will fast unfold,
A Christmas wonder few have seen and fewer have been told:
The Church of the Nativity will host a joyous rite,
As little angels gather on this holiest of nights.

The cherubim assemble to observe our Saviour's birth;
This annual tradition brings a celebrated mirth!
But first, before the merriment begins, each Yuletide,
The angels seek a moment that they've never been denied.

Atop the walls, they're lined and waiting silently, serene,
Their forms, of near transparence, keep the multitude unseen;
Collectively, they gaze toward the belfry, strong and white,
Patiently awaiting their expected thrill this night.

Then from the silence cradling the church this holy eve,
A stirring's heard – it's just enough for angels to perceive;
Below the ropes that hang beneath the tower's golden bells,
Little cherubs have appeared, and how the rapture swells!

They grasp the ropes - with all their might, the little cherubs heave,
Then one by one and up and down their little bodies weave;
The clappers strike inside the bells and peal a gift, profound,
With clarity and melody – a wondrous Christmas sound!

And then the angels from the walls arise and whirl about;
They soar and sway and swirl, with euphoria throughout!
Their Christmas gift has now arrived, such revelling ensues!
With cheerfulness they celebrate their yearly rendezvous.

Flinging, still, the cherubs in their gowns, are smiling so,
They barely keep their sandals on while swinging to and fro;
Their laughter joins the music, blending with the bells they ring,
While all the other angels cheer the blessings that they bring!

Then overhead, the angels take position row on row.
And blending with the bells, a gentle murmur starts to grow;
It's soft, but so melodious, and what a gift to bring –
The angels sing a song of worship to the newborn King!

And then…the cherubs leave the ropes to dangle free once more;
They disappear – the ringing fades to silence, as before.
There's stillness in the belfry, just as earlier this night,
Before the cherubs brought their yearly gift of pure delight!

And with a whirr, the angels, too, to Heaven take their leave,
Oh, what a time of merriment they had on Christmas Eve!
Surely Heaven's holding them throughout the blessed morn',
So, with the cherubs, they can praise that Christ the Lord is born.

CHRISTMAS PRAYER

Dear Lord
On this lovely, holy Eve,
Be with me, I pray
And guide me to understand your coming,
And why it is we celebrate, especially now.

Help me to look beyond the presents and their flowing ribbons;
Open my heart and my eyes, and help me to see and feel
The suffering that shakes our Earth.
Many hunger, and are cold and lonely
In this world of plenty;
And many stray from your light, by evil and its ways.
And the hustle and bustle,
How I fear it's replaced the real joy we should feel.

That starry night so long ago
So quietly, peacefully, you entered our world
And through your love, your guidance, your sacrifice
You taught us to be good and kind to one another - to everyone.

Help us to look inside ourselves
To find you,
So that together, we may bring true happiness and peace
To everyone.
Help us to look beyond ourselves
So that we may embrace our world, and ease the pain.

Thy night is silent;
Thy night is holy.
Lord, Bless everyone with the joyful calmness of
Your arrival.
Amen.

ABOUT THE AUTHOR

Derek grew up in a family of 10, so Christmas gatherings were always busy, but fun.

"Some of my most precious memories of Christmas include:
The growing anticipation throughout the Advent season;
Mom's delicious and aromatic baking, and the way she made the interior of our house look so festive;
Dad's outdoor decorating – placing the nativity figures in just the right place in the front yard, and the lights lined up neatly on the house, fences, and trees, all around the property;
The many Christmas albums that played such beautiful music on Mom and Dad's old stereo;
Dad's effortlessly skillful guitar accompaniment while both he and Mom led us in singing carols on Christmas Eve;
The excitement of Christmas Eve day, ending with attending the Christmas Eve Midnight Mass, arriving early enough to sing along with the carols sung before Mass started;
The excitement, joy, and love that were shared in our living room on Christmas morning;
The many late nights of playing cards and board games with both family and friends, with much laughter and merriment.

"Through all of this, it was the joyous message of the season – the celebration of the birth of our Saviour – that remained the focal point of each of those Christmas moments and memories, and the inspiration for this collection of writings."

Derek Becher

www.ingramcontent.com/pod-product-compliance
Lightning Source LLC
Chambersburg PA
CBHW060508030426
42337CB00015B/1789